D0432388

385.
312

London
North of the Thames

Colin and David McCarthy

Ian Allan
PUBLISHING

Contents

Previous page: This and the photograph on page 71 record the dramatic changes wrought at Euston following its controversial rebuilding in the early 1960s. This first view, taken in the early 1960s, records the original station prior to work commencing on its demolition.
British Railways

First published 2009

ISBN 978 0 7110 3346 7

All rights reserved. No part of this book may be reproduced or transmitted in any form or by any means, electronic or mechanical, including photocopying, recording, scanning or by any information storage and retrieval system, on the internet or elsewhere, without permission from the Publisher in writing.

© Colin McCarthy, David McCarthy and Michael Cobb 2009

Published by Ian Allan Publishing
an imprint of Ian Allan Publishing Ltd, Hersham, Surrey KT12 4RG.
Printed in England by Ian Allan Printing Ltd, Hersham, Surrey KT12 4RG.

Visit the Ian Allan Publishing website at www.ianallanpublishing.com

Copyright
Illegal copying and selling of publications deprives authors, publishers and booksellers of income, without which there would be no investment in new publications. Unauthorised versions of publications are also likely to be inferior in quality and contain incorrect information. You can help by reporting copyright infringements and acts of piracy to the Publisher or the UK Copyright Service.

In 2003 Colonel Michael Cobb published his superb two-volume atlas covering the railways of Great Britain. This work, widely praised when first published and subsequently reprinted and then reissued as a revised second edition, forms the basis of the cartography in this, the fourth of a new series that is designed to provide a comprehensive historical guide to the railways of the country.

The cartography shows the railway infrastructure of the area concerned, differentiating the lines built between those open for passenger services, those open for freight only, those preserved and those closed completely. Alongside the railways, the major roads of the area are also shown so that readers can identify the inter-relationship between road and rail transport.

When compiling his original books Michael Cobb decided to exclude those lines that were not constructed by the main-line companies; these tended to be predominantly industrial, the intention here being to incorporate as many of these as possible. Also included is an indication of locomotive sheds, fuller details of which can be found in the book's narrative.

Supplementing the cartography, the book also includes an outline history of the lines featured supported by a representative selection of photographs portraying the railway locations discussed. The book concludes with a full gazetteer of all the stations featured, giving opening and closing dates, as well as information about renaming if appropriate.

Notes on the maps

The maps are based upon the original work undertaken by Col Cobb for his atlas; individual symbols are described within the key. The railway routes shown are differentiated between the lines that are open to passenger services (split between those that form part of the National Network, those that form part of the London Underground and those of the Docklands Light Railway), those that are open to freight traffic only, preserved lines and those closed completely. Station names with earlier versions are given; fuller details of the opening and closing dates of the stations can be found in the comprehensive index and gazetteer included at the back of the book. The major road network is shown as a means of placing the open and closed lines into their local context; the book, however, is not a road atlas and therefore minor roads are excluded. It should also be noted that the road network shown is the contemporary one, in order to demonstrate the inter-relationship between the existing and closed railways with the modern road system. In a number of places a closed railway may well have been used in whole or in part for the realignment of the road after closure. In addition, 'road crossings' may have been added as a result of the construction of new roads, where none existed when the railway was extant. If on the level (*i.e.* without the construction of a new bridge) these are indicated by the level-crossing symbol; this is not to suggest, however, that a level crossing existed there whilst the railway was operational.

ondon's railway network north of the River Thames is probably the most complex in the country. Inevitably, as the country's capital city and one of the major industrial, commercial and maritime centres, London was to be the focus for many of the earliest railway schemes – such as the London & Birmingham, the London & Blackwall, the Eastern Counties and the Great Western – but the rapid growth of the city and its environs – the population of the whole of London rose from 959,000 in 1801 to 1,655,000 in 1831, to 2,363,000 in 1851 and to 6,506,000 in 1901 (with much of the growth during the earlier years being north of the river) – was to see massive investment both during the 19th century and subsequently.

At the dawn of the railway age the new stations opened by the pioneering companies – such as Euston, Paddington and Bishopsgate – represented the outer limits of the heavily built-up areas; there were settlements beyond these stations but the 19th century is largely a story of the rapid expansion of London itself as it gradually swallowed up these outlying towns and villages. Although the railways determined to try and serve the central area this was largely impractical until the development of electric traction made possible the construction and operation of the Tube network. The early lines that were later to form part of the Underground network – such as the Metropolitan – skirted round the central core of the city rather than penetrating it; it was only after 1890 that the first deep-level Tubes opened, allowing the City and West End finally to be connected to the railway network.

Apart from being the country's primary financial centre London was also the country's primary port and, during the 19th century (reflecting Britain's pre-eminence both as an industrial power house and as the centre of a growing empire), the area occupied by the docks grew massively. The first of the Georgian docks was the West India (opened 1802), followed by the London (1805), East India (also 1805), Surrey (1807), St Katharine's (1828) and West India South (1829). The Victorian docks were mostly further east, comprising the Royal Victoria (1855), Millwall (1868) and Royal Albert (1880). The King George V was a late addition, in 1921. In order to serve these docks a network of lines was provided and the traffic generated by the docks – both passenger and freight – stimulated lines such as the North London.

Whilst London is now perceived very much as a single entity, for the first century of the capital's railway development the London area was formed of myriad local authorities. As a result the promotion of lines was not centrally planned but based upon the aspirations of the individual railway promoters; this lack of co-ordinated activity was to lead to some duplication of services – albeit not as significant as elsewhere in the country, and generally the population growth, particularly in the suburbs (which led to the increase in commuter traffic encouraged by the concept, for example, of Metroland), ensured that traffic often followed the opening of new lines. It was, however, not until the creation of the London Passenger Transport Board (and its successors) in 1933 that, for the first time, did the Greater London area have a body capable of undertaking the strategic planning necessary for the efficient provision of public transport.

Since the 1930s there has been ongoing investment in London's railway network, although not all the plans proposed have ultimately come to fruition. The ambitious New Works Programme of the 1930s was only partially implemented prior to the outbreak of World War 2, and the subsequent period of austerity resulted in a number of schemes being delayed or cancelled. The integration of a number of the ex-LNER lines into the Underground network undoubtedly benefited commuters and travellers from Essex and from north Middlesex, whilst the Underground network itself has expanded via new lines – the Victoria and Jubilee – and the extension of the Piccadilly Line to serve Heathrow Airport. Moreover, reflecting the changing base of London's economy as a result of the decline of the docks and other traditional industries has seen further significant investment, most notably in the construction of the Docklands Light Railway. In the first decades of the 21st century there are further significant developments to note with the opening in 2007 of the high-speed line serving St Pancras International, whilst after years of delay work has finally commenced on the Crossrail project. Elsewhere the creation of the London Overground network and the incorporation within it of an extended East London Line sees the reuse of previously abandoned infrastructure.

London as a city needs an efficient railway network to function properly; through the pages of this book it is possible to see how the early piecemeal development of the area's railway system has evolved over time into a network that can today handle the millions that make use of it annually.

Left: Forming a service from Lewisham, DLR B-2-B units Nos 31 and 64 arrive at their Canary Wharf destination on 25 March 2009.
Brian Morrison

Baker Street & Waterloo Railway

This three-mile electrified line was incorporated on 28 March 1893 in order to provide Waterloo with a connection into the West End, while two mile-long extensions – to Paddington and to Elephant & Castle – were authorised on 6 August 1900. The line from Kennington Road (now Lambeth Road) opened on 10 April 1906, extensions being opened from Kennington Road to Elephant & Castle on 5 August 1906, from Baker Street to Marylebone on 17 March 1907, and from Marylebone to Edgware Road on 15 June. Following an Act dated 26 July 1910 the BS&WJR was incorporated into the London Electric Railway. The extension from Edgware Road to Paddington was opened on 1 December 1913. Along with other sections of the Tube network the line, now part of the Bakerloo, passed to the London Passenger Transport Board in 1933.

One of the most important intermediate stations on the Bakerloo Line and one of the few tube stations where trains pass in such close proximity is Piccadilly Circus, seen here on 16 March 1983. Viewed from the northbound platform, a southbound train formed of 1938 stock stands at the platform. *John Glover*

Becontree Estate Railway

Begun in 1921, Becontree was the flagship of the London County Council's 'cottage estate' house-building programme and was intended to accommodate 100,000 people. To facilitate its construction a standard-gauge steam-operated railway line was laid from Chadwell Heath station, via temporary bridges over existing lines, to the Thames, where a 500ft-long jetty was constructed to handle raw materials brought up the river. The railway was to survive until 1934.

Birmingham, Bristol & Thames Junction Railway

Empowered on 21 June 1836 to construct a line from the Thames to connect with both the Great Western and London & Birmingham railways, the company's name was changed in 1840 to the West London Railway.

Brompton & Piccadilly Circus Railway

The B&PCR was incorporated on 6 August 1897 and empowered to construct the 2¾-mile line from Earl's Court to Piccadilly. The proposed line came under the control of Charles Yerkes' Underground Group in 1901 and on 8 August 1902 was merged with another constituent of the group, the Great Northern & Strand, to become the Great Northern, Piccadilly & Brompton Railway.

Central London Railway

One of a number of competing schemes for the construction of an underground line from Shepherd's Bush into the city, the CLR was incorporated on 5 August 1891 to construct a line from Wood Lane to Bank. The line from Shepherd's Bush to Bank opened on 30 July 1900, the western extension to Wood Lane opening on 14 May 1908. Initially the line was operated using electric

Left: At the sharply curved platform at Bank, a westbound Central Line train formed of 1959 stock calls en route to Ealing Broadway in February 1986. *Colin Boocock*

Left: A Hainault-bound train formed of 1962 stock approaches White City on 11 January 1975. *Kevin Lane*

Right: Bound for Epping, a Central Line train calls at North Acton station on 21 February 1976. *Kevin Lane*

Right: The view east at Ealing Broadway, showing the complex track arrangements at the station. The two lines on the extreme left form the District Line route to Turnham Green; the electrified lines in the foreground (right) are those of the Central Line heading towards North Acton, whilst on the extreme right, in the background, are the non-electrified tracks of the ex-GWR main line out of Paddington. The train arriving is a District Line service formed of 'D' stock. The ex-GWR main line would be electrified subsequently for operation of the Heathrow Express services. *John Glover*

locomotives but these proved problematic and were soon replaced by multiple-unit operation. An eastward extension to Liverpool Street, originally authorised on 28 June 1892, was finally opened on 28 July 1912. On 3 August 1920 the line was further extended, this time from Wood Lane to Ealing Broadway. The CLR became part of the LPTB on 1 July 1933 and today forms part of the Central Line.

Channel Tunnel Rail Link

Authorised by the Channel Tunnel Rail Link Act of 1996, the CTRL was designed to provide a fast link between London and the Channel Tunnel. The line was completed in two phases: that from the Channel Tunnel to Fawkham Junction, in North Kent, was opened on 28 September 2003 and the second, from Ebbsfleet to St Pancras via Stratford was to follow on 14 November 2007. The second phase is some 24 miles in length and includes one intermediate station at Stratford. The completion of the CTRL saw Eurostar rolling stock transferred from North Pole Depot to a new maintenance facility at Temple Mills as well as the massive £800 million redevelopment of St Pancras station into the new St Pancras International.

Below: Beneath the superbly restored Barlow trainshed at St Pancras International two rakes of Eurostar stock await their next duty on 10 December 2007. *Brian Morrison*

Above: Heralding a service that would start a year later, Class 395 'Javelin' No 395002 stands at St Pancras International's Platform 13 on 12 December 2008. Just visible on the right, at Platform 11, is a Eurostar.
Brian Morrison

Right: On 13 April 1983 a southbound train formed of 1959 stock arrives at Charing Cross station with a service for Kennington. The David Gentleman graphic panels, a feature of the station, that record the construction of the original cross built to mark the death of Queen Eleanor, can be seen on the left.
John Glover

Charing Cross, Euston & Hampstead Railway

Now part of the Northern Line, the CCE&HR was one of a number of schemes proposed after the success of the City & South London. Although authorised initially on 24 August 1893, it was not until 1900, when American financier Charles Tyson Yerkes bought the powers, that progress was made under the auspices of the Metropolitan District Electric Traction Co Ltd, which had been founded on 15 July 1901. This company was reconstituted in 1902 as the Underground Electric Railways Co of London. Work on constructing the CCE&HR line commenced in September 1903 and the line was opened from

the Strand – now Charing Cross station – to Golders Green with the branch from Camden Town to Highgate – now known as Archway – on 22 January 1907. The company was absorbed by the London Electric Railway following an Act of 27 July 1910. The line was extended south from the Strand to Embankment – then known as Charing Cross – on 6 April 1914 and thence to a connection with the City & South London at Kennington on 13 September 1926. The connection with the City & South London, with its complex junction, had opened on 20 April 1924.

Charing Cross Railway

The Charing Cross Railway, a two-mile extension from London Bridge via Waterloo East to Charing Cross, was incorporated on 8 August 1859 and, costing some £4 million, was opened on 11 January 1864. The CCR was taken over by the South Eastern Railway on 1 August 1864 and thus became part of the SR in 1923. The line remains open, passenger services now being provided by the South Eastern franchise.

City & South London Railway

Now part of the Northern Line (City Branch), the C&SLR had its origins in the City of London & Southwark Subway Co, which was authorised in 1884 to construct a 1¼-mile cable-operated line from King William Street to Elephant &

Castle. Powers to extend the line south from Elephant & Castle to Stockwell, a further 1¾ miles, were obtained in 1887. In 1888 it was announced that electric, rather than cable, traction would be used and, two years later, a further southern extension to Clapham Common – opened on 3 June 1900 – was authorised. The line opened from King William Street to Stockwell on 18 December 1890. However, the King William Street terminus proved inadequate and powers were obtained for the construction of a new alignment from Borough through the City to Moorgate; this opened on 25 February 1900 and resulted in the closure of the line from King William Street to Borough. Further expansion to the north saw the line extended to Angel on 17 November 1901 and to Euston via King's Cross on 12 May 1907. The line was rebuilt between 1922 and 1924 to permit the use of standard Tube stock to operate over it. The C&SLR remained independent until it was incorporated into the LPTB on 1 July 1933.

Below: On 5 November 1988 passengers board and alight from a Morden-bound train at Angel station. This was the last of the stations on the line to be formed of a single island platform; shortly after the date of the photograph work would start on a major project to modernise the station, including the creation of two separate platforms for north- and southbound services. *Kevin Lane*

Commercial Railway

Authorised on 28 July 1836, the 5ft 0in-gauge CR was empowered to construct the 3¼-mile line from the Minories to Blackwall in order to improve communications between Brunswick Wharf and the City. On 17 August 1839 a 415yd extension to Fenchurch Street was authorised and the company changed its name to London & Blackwall.

Docklands Light Railway

Intended as a means of helping the regeneration of the London docklands, the first phase of the DLR, built between 1985 and 1987, opened on 31 August 1987 and linked Tower Gateway with Stratford and Island Gardens. The initial network was eight kilometres in length but was soon to be extended. The first extension saw the line reach further into the city, opening to Bank on 29 July 1991. This was followed by the Beckton line from Poplar, opened on 28 March 1994. The next extension saw the DLR extended south of the river upon the opening of the line south from Island Gardens to Lewisham. The new line saw the original stations at Mudchute and Island Gardens replaced as it descended to pass under the river in a tunnel. This line opened on 3 December 1999. A further extension was opened on 2 December 2005, running from Canning Town to King George VI via London City Airport; this line was extended under the river to a new terminus at Woolwich Arsenal on 10 January 2009. In late 2007 the erstwhile Network Rail line from Stratford to North Woolwich was closed; the next extension for DLR, scheduled to open in 2010, will see the system extended north from Canning Town over the route of the closed North Woolwich line to serve both Stratford and Stratford International stations.

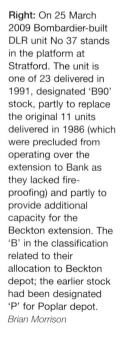

Right: On 25 March 2009 Bombardier-built DLR unit No 37 stands in the platform at Stratford. The unit is one of 23 delivered in 1991, designated 'B90' stock, partly to replace the original 11 units delivered in 1986 (which were precluded from operating over the extension to Bank as they lacked fire-proofing) and partly to provide additional capacity for the Beckton extension. The 'B' in the classification related to their allocation to Beckton depot; the earlier stock had been designated 'P' for Poplar depot.
Brian Morrison

Ealing & South Harrow Railway

Incorporated on 25 June 1894, the E&SHR, now part of the contemporary Piccadilly Line, was empowered to construct a five-mile line from Hanger Lane Junction to South Harrow. Having been used as a test track for electric trains to Park Royal for the Royal Show of 23-27 June 1903 – the section was the first part of the future Underground network's surface route to be electrified – the line was opened throughout to South Harrow on 28 June 1903. Originally it had been intended that the line would be operated by the District Railway following an Act of 26 March 1900 but was vested in the Metropolitan District Railway following an Act of 6 August 1900. The line became part of the Piccadilly Line on 4 July 1932 upon the transfer of the section from the District Line. The MDR passed to the LPTB on 1 July 1933.

East & West India Docks & Birmingham Junction Railway

Forerunner of the North London Railway – the shorter name was adopted on 1 January 1853 – the LNWR-backed railway was empowered following an Act of 26 August 1846 to construct a line from Poplar and the docks to Camden and a connection with the LNWR. The first section, from Bow Junction, on the London & Blackwall, to Islington opened on 26 September 1850; this was extended to Camden Town (later Chalk Road) on 7 December 1850 (coal traffic started on 20 October 1851) and to Hampstead Road (later Chalk Farm) on 9 June 1851. The line was extended southwards from Bow Junction to Poplar on 1 January 1852 and was quadrupled between Camden Town and Dalston Junction in 1871. Passenger services over the line from Dalston Junction to Poplar (East India Road) were withdrawn on 15 April 1944 (although a substitute bus operated until

Left: The exterior of Bow station proudly proclaims its North London Railway ownership. The original station opened in 1850 but the structure here dates to the early 1870s when the NLR undertook the rebuilding of a number of its stations to the design of E. H. Horne. Bow station was to close towards the end of World War 2, although a new station – Bow Church – was opened on the same site in 1987 to serve the new Docklands Light Railway. *Ian Allan Library*

13

Above: A Cravens-built two-car DMU heads east at Canonbury Junction on 16 May 1979 on the 11.24 service from Camden Road to North Woolwich. The line curving to the north from the junction is the 1874 link to Finsbury Park that saw passenger services from 1875 until 1976.
Les Bertram

23 April 1945). However, passenger services over the section from Dalston Junction to Victoria Park Junction were reintroduced on 12 May 1980 as part of the process of the gradual withdrawal of services to Broad Street and the re-routing of NLR services to terminate at North Woolwich. The line south from Victoria Park Junction via Bow Junction to Poplar Docks was finally to close on 3 October 1983. However, the section of this route between Bow Junction and Poplar was reopened as part of the new Docklands Light Railway on 31 August 1987.

East London Railway

Incorporated on 26 May 1865 to provide a link between the London, Brighton & South Coast, Great Eastern and South Eastern railways, the ELR was empowered to utilise the pedestrian tunnel built originally by Marc and Isambard Brunel between 1824 and 1843 – the first crossing under the Thames. The line opened from Wapping to New Cross (now New Cross Gate) on 7 December 1869. Extensions were opened from Rotherhithe to Old Kent Road on 13 March 1871 (although this closed on 1 June 1911), from Wapping to Shoreditch on 10 April 1876 and to New Cross on 1 April 1880. The line was operated by the LBSCR from opening but subsequently services were also provided by the SER and GER. Following the City Line Act of 1879, a connection was made with the Metropolitan and District railways at Whitechapel, services over the new line commencing on 6 October 1884. The line was electrified in 1913, the last steam-operated services running on 30 March 1913. Thereafter the Metropolitan was the sole operator. Passenger

Left: The northern terminus of the Underground's East London Line was Shoreditch; this station closed in 2006 upon the commencement of work to convert the East London Line into part of the expanded London Overground network. On 9 February 1978 the driver spills his cup of tea as he walks to the front of the train prior to returning south to Whitechapel and New Cross. *John Glover*

services over the curve at Whitechapel linking the ELR with the rest of the Metropolitan were withdrawn in 1941, the line being retained thereafter for stock transfers only. For the remainder of its life as part of the Tube network the ELR line operated generally from Whitechapel to New Cross/New Cross Gate, the section north to Shoreditch being used solely at peak hours. Ownership of the line, which had passed to the Southern Railway in 1925, was transferred to the London Transport Executive in 1948. In 2001, following several years of discussion, the go-ahead was given to the modernisation and extension of the line. North of the river the project sees it diverted from Shoreditch – where the original station closed on 9 June 2006 – to run over the erstwhile NLR route north of Broad Street to Dalston Junction and its incorporation within the London Overground network. In order to achieve this passenger services were suspended on the ELR in 2007, and the new line is scheduled to reopen in 2010.

Eastern Counties Railway

Authorised on 4 July 1836, the ECR was empowered to construct the 126-mile main line from Norwich to London to a gauge of 5ft 0in, although ultimately it failed to build the line east of Colchester. The first section to open, linking Devonshire Street (Mile End), located just to the east of Bethnal Green, with Romford, came into use on 20 June 1839. The line was extended both eastwards – to Brentford – and westwards – to Shoreditch (known as Bishopsgate from 1846) – on 1 July 1840, the route through to Colchester opening for freight traffic on 7 March 1843 and to passengers on 29 March. The line was converted to standard gauge in late 1844. The company grew through the leasing of the Northern & Eastern Railway on 1 January 1844 and through the acquisition of companies in Norfolk and Suffolk, becoming the Great Eastern Railway on 7 August 1862. Apart from the short stretch into Bishopsgate – a station that was converted into a goods yard following closure to passenger services on 1 November 1875 and closed following a fire on 5 December 1964 – the remainder of the ex-ECR main line, now electrified (originally at 1,500V DC, opening as such on 26 September 1949, but converted to 6.25kV in 1960 and to 25kV in the late 1970s), remains open as part of the London–Norwich main line, services now being provided by National Express East Anglia. Apart from the main line the ECR also constructed a number of other lines, including:

Silvertown–Thames Wharf Junction

This line was opened on 1 December 1855 and allowed for the diversion of passenger services from the North Woolwich Railway. In 1880, as a result of the opening of the King Albert Dock, the passenger line was diverted through the short Connaught Tunnel, although the original surface line remained open for freight traffic until 18 April 1966. From 1866 to 1874 the Great Eastern and NLR operated the line in alternate years before the GER took over sole operation. Steam traction was replaced by diesel in 1963. The route was extended on to the North London Line in 1979 and, in 1985, converted from diesel to third-rail electric trains, which then ran an extended route from North Woolwich round inner north London to Richmond. The line was singled from Custom House to North Woolwich. In 1994 the Beckton extension of the Docklands Light Railway was opened; this ran parallel to the branch from Tidal Basin through to the west of the entrance to Connaught Tunnel. Passenger services over the branch were latterly

Right: On 17 June 1939 work is in progress to the east of Stratford station in connection with the planned extension of the Central Line from Liverpool Street. Although work was well advanced by the outbreak of World War 2, it would not be until the late 1940s that the project would be finally completed.
Ian Allan Library

Left: A photograph taken at Leytonstone on 14 July 1947 records the transitional period when electric services had been extended as far as Leytonstone but steam continued to power services onwards to Epping and Ongar. A Central Line train can be seen in the platform, whilst Class N7/1 No 9658 awaits departure with a service to Epping. *A. F. Cook*

operated by Silverlink but the line from Stratford to North Woolwich was closed on 9 December 2006 to allow for the conversion of the section from Canning Town to Stratford as part of an expanded DLR. The section from Canning Town to North Woolwich closed completely on that date. There are plans for the conversion of the closed section to form part of a new heritage line.

Stratford–Loughton

The seven-mile line opened from Loughton Branch Junction to Loughton on 22 August 1856. The line was extended a further 11½ miles to Ongar, via Epping, on 24 April 1865. In the mid-1930s it was decided to incorporate the branch with an eastward extension of the Central Line; although work started, it was not until after World War 2 that London Transport electric services were progressively introduced. Central Line services from Stratford to Leytonstone were introduced on 5 May 1947, being extended to Woodford on 14 December

Left: On 1 March 1977 the 11.10 service from North Woolwich to Stratford Low Level calls at Custom House (Victoria Dock) station. The open window of the driver's cab signifies that he has just surrendered the single-line token – all passenger trains used the erstwhile down line between Custom House and Silvertown and in the distance the line can be seen curving down onto the incline towards Connaught Tunnel. The line towards Beckton, that survived as a stub at this point, headed due east from Custom House.
John Glovert

Below: The northern
terminus of EC&TJR was
originally Stratford, the
link opening to the North
London line at Victoria
Park in 1854. This was
the view north at Stratford
Low Level on 16 May
1979, with two Cravens-
built DMUs passing. The
relationship between the
high- and low-level
platforms at the station
is evident, as is the
proximity of the site to the
buildings of Stratford
diesel depot in the
background. This scene
is now radically altered
following the demolition
of the depot, the
electrification of the ex-
GER main line, the arrival
of both the Docklands
Light Railway and the
Jubilee Line extension,
and the withdrawal of the
DMU service from
Stratford to North
Woolwich. *Les Bertram*

1947, thence to Loughton on 21 November 1948. Electric services were
introduced between Loughton and Epping on 25 September 1949 but were not
to be extended from Epping to Ongar until 18 November 1957. Freight services
operated by the LNER and BR survived over the line until the 1960s and there
remained a number of early morning peak services that ran from Epping over
the main-line connection until 1970. The short line from Loughton Branch
Junction to Leyton closed completely on 1 June 1970 and was removed two
years later. After some years of decline the line between Epping and Ongar
closed completely on 30 September 1994; the route is now preserved as the
Epping–Ongar Railway.

Eastern Counties & Thames Junction Railway

Promoted by G. P. Bidder, this was incorporated on 4 July 1844 to construct a
1¾-mile line from Stratford, on the Eastern Counties Railway, to Thames
Wharf, on Barking Creek. Built by the ECR, the line was opened on 19 April
1846 and was extended to North Woolwich via the North Woolwich Railway.
Bidder operated passenger services over the route until 1854, when the North
London Railway took over; from 1866 to 1874 the Great Eastern and NLR
operated the line in alternate years before the GER took over sole operation.
Passenger services were operated latterly by Silverlink, but the line from
Stratford to North Woolwich was closed on 9 December 2006 to allow the
section from Canning Town to Stratford to be converted to become part of an
expanded Docklands Light Railway; on the same date the section from Canning
Town to North Woolwich closed completely.

Edgware & Hampstead Railway

Incorporated on 18 November 1902, the E&HR saw its powers transferred on 7 August 1912 to the London Electric Railway. The line was finally opened on 19 November 1923.

Edgeware, Highgate & London Railway

Incorporated on 3 June 1862, the railway – with its mis-spelt first name – was authorised to construct an 8¾-mile branch from Seven Sisters (Finsbury Park) to Edgware. Sponsored by the GNR, the EH&LR was taken over by the larger concern on 15 July 1867 shortly prior to the line's opening on 22 August 1867.

Left: Pictured in 1928, an ex-GNR condensing tank stands at the head of a service to Finchley (Church End). Passenger services between West Finchley and Edgware ceased in 1939 with the intention that the line be incorporated within an extended Northern Line; in the event, passenger services were never reintroduced west of Mill Hill East and the line to Edgware was to close completely upon the withdrawal of freight traffic in 1964. *Ian Allan Library*

Left: After the line from Highgate to Finsbury Park was closed for freight traffic, the route was retained for the transfer of stock from Highgate depot to the Northern City branch. Here, in June 1968, a four-car rake of 1938 stock is pictured at the closed Crouch End station being hauled by battery locomotive No 21 en route to the depot. *K. Harris*

Above: In 1983 north- and southbound trains, both formed of 1959 stock, stand awaiting departure from Finchley Central station. Until 1962 the station was served by a goods yard, the site of which was on the extreme right of the photograph behind the fence. *John Glover*

In 1864 powers were obtained to extend it from Edgware to Watford but these were allowed to lapse. As with the rest of the GNR's network of lines in the 'Northern Heights' the passenger service was quite intense by the start of the 20th century as population growth led to increased commuter traffic. However, by the 1920s the effect of the gradient from Finsbury Park to Park Junction (Highgate), allied to the growing competition from electric trams and later trolleybuses, meant that the steam-hauled service was increasingly unreliable. In 1935 plans were drawn up to transfer the entire 'Northern Heights' network to the LPTB and integrate the lines into an expanded Underground system. With the Northern Line extended from Archway, electric services commenced operation over the section of the EH&LR from East to West Finchley on 14 April 1940. Passenger services over the line from West Finchley to Edgware were suspended on 11 September 1939 in order to facilitate conversion; in the event electric services to Mill Hill East were inaugurated on 18 May 1941, but work on the line to Edgware was suspended and, in February 1954, formally abandoned. Although passenger services were now restricted to the section from Mill Hill East to East Finchley, the LNER (and later BR) continued to operate freight traffic over the line. The section from Mill Hill East to Edgware was to close finally upon the withdrawal of freight facilities in 1964. The section from Finsbury Park to Park Junction, retained to facilitate transfer of stock from Highgate Wood depot to the Northern City Line from 4 May 1964, closed completely on 5 May 1970 and was lifted two years later.

Gas Light & Coke Co

Following the construction of a gasworks adjacent to the River Thames at Beckton the GL&CC constructed a 1¾-mile branch from Albert Dock Junction, on the North Woolwich line, to Beckton. Leased to the GER, the line opened for freight traffic on 14 October 1872, a passenger service being introduced with effect from 17 March 1873. In 1911 there were five return workings per weekday, with trains operating through to Stratford Market (taking some 20min for the 4¾-mile journey), with two return workings on Sundays. Passenger services, which had declined to one return working by the end, were withdrawn on 28 December 1940. The line was to close completely on 22 February 1971 following the closure of the gasworks. At the eastern end, part of the 1994 extension to the Docklands Light Railway to Beckton runs parallel to the original line.

Great Central Railway

Empowered following an Act of 28 March 1893, the Manchester, Sheffield & Lincolnshire Railway's London Extension was designed to link with the Metropolitan at Quainton Road. From Harrow-on-the-Hill it headed towards the new terminus at Marylebone along tracks separate from but parallel to those of the Metropolitan. On 1 August 1897 the MS&LR changed its name to the Great Central and, on 26 July 1898, coal traffic started running over the route. Passenger services commenced on 15 March 1899 and general freight traffic on 11 April 1899. A second route to the north – courtesy of the Great Western & Great Central Joint – saw the GC open the line from Northolt Junction to Neasden on 1 March 1906. Both sections of ex-GCR route passed to the LNER in 1923 and to BR in 1948; today passenger services over the lines are provided by Chiltern Railways.

Left: An unidentified BR Standard Class 5 4-6-0 emerges from Lords Tunnel on the climb out of Marylebone with the 2.38pm service to Nottingham during the first week of July 1964. *R. L. Sewell*

Right: On 29 July 1981 a Derby-built Class 115 four-car DMU departs Harrow-on-the-Hill station with the 12.10 service from Marylebone to Aylesbury. *Brian Morrison*

Great Eastern Railway

This was formed on 7 August 1862 and incorporated amongst others the Eastern Counties Railway. A limited number of lines in the London area were promoted or constructed. These included:

Palace Gates branch

The 2¼-mile branch from Seven Sisters to Palace Gates opened in two stages: from the junction at Seven Sisters to Green Lanes (on 1 January 1878) and thence to Palace Gates on 7 October the same year. In 1929 a connection was laid at Palace Gates northwards to link into the ex-GNR Hertford loop line but this was not fully signalled until 1944, after which it was used for freight traffic and occasional excursions from the GN section to Southend. A coal-concentration depot was established to the north of Palace Gates station in 1954. Passenger services over the branch were withdrawn on 7 January 1963, and the original branch closed completely on 28 December 1964. The coal-concentration depot survived until 1984 and the northernmost part of the 1929 connection is now incorporated within Bounds Green depot.

Liverpool Street

On 17 December 1862 the GER's then engineer and chief engineer recommended the extension of the line to a new terminus closer to the City. This recommendation was accepted, and on 31 December 1863 the Great Eastern Metropolitan Station & Railways Co was formed. The new station was opened for suburban traffic on 2 February 1874 and completely on 1 November 1875 (when the existing terminus at Bishopsgate was closed and converted into a goods shed).

Fairlop Loop

This 6¼-mile line, from a triangular junction at Ilford to a junction with the line to Ongar at Woodford, was opened on 1 May 1903. In the mid-1930s it was proposed that part of the route be incorporated within an extended Central Line but it was not until after World War 2 that these plans were completed. LNER passenger services over the line from Ilford to Woodford were withdrawn on 30 November 1947, to be replaced by a temporary bus service. Electric services were introduced from Newbury Park to Hainault on 31 May 1948 and thence to Woodford on 21 November 1948. The section south from Newbury Park to Seven Kings remained open for freight traffic until complete closure on 19 March 1956; the curve from Ilford towards Newbury Park closed upon the withdrawal of passenger services in 1947, and part of the new Ilford EMU depot was built on the trackbed.

Left: Post-Nationalisation, Class L1 2-6-4T No 67724 is recorded about to push the empty stock from the 1.27pm Saturdays Only arrival from North Woolwich into the carriage sidings at Palace Gates.
M. A. Schumann

Left: Along with the original ECR line to Epping, plans were formulated for the conversion of the Fairlop Loop as part of an extended Central Line in the 1930s, but not until the late 1940s would work on the Loop be completed. This view, recorded at Hainault in 1982, shows a train formed of 1960 stock heading for Woodford and a train of 1962 stock arriving at the station. *John Glover*

Right: Brush Type 2 No 5627 is pictured about to plunge into the darkness of Copenhagen Tunnel with a down train on 22 March 1973.
Brian Morrison

Great Northern Railway

Incorporated on 26 June 1846, this ambitious scheme was to construct the southern section of the future East Coast main line from London to York. The line opened from Maiden Lane (London) to Peterborough on 7 August 1850. The railway's London terminus – King's Cross – opened on 14 October 1852. On 1 October 1863 a connection was opened between the GNR main line and the Metropolitan Railway to Farringdon. On 1 January 1866 a station – on the site of the King's Cross York Road platform – was opened on the East Curve to

Right: With the exception of the short section through Welwyn North, the opportunity was taken during the late 1950s to quadruple the ex-GNR main line. Here, on 1 October 1959, a four-car suburban DMU is recorded departing from Hadley Wood over the newly completed four-line section.
British Railways

Left: Electric services at 25kV over the ex-GNR main line from Finsbury Park to Welwyn Garden City and Hertford North were launched on 8 November 1976. Here, on 14 September 1978, a Moorgate–Hertford North service approaches Wood Green station, with Class 313 No 313012 leading. *John Glover*

serve trains originating from the Snow Hill route; it was not until 1 February 1878 that a platform serving the Hotel Curve on the west was opened. The services to and from Farringdon and the LC&DR were steam-hauled until the suburban services were 'dieselised' on 23 March. The two curves remained open until closure on 8 November 1976 (except for a brief reprieve for York Road between 1 March and 5 March 1977 in connection with the simplification of the track layout and the electrification of the line at King's Cross), when the DMU service was withdrawn, ultimately to be replaced by the electrified service than rat to Luton and Bedford. The main line, now fully electrified, sees East Coast services provided mainly (at the time of writing) by National Express, suburban services and those to East Anglia being provided by First Capital Connect.

Great Northern & City Railway

Backed by the GNR, the GN&CR was incorporated on 28 June 1892 to construct a line from the Canonbury curve to Moorgate. However, rather than form a junction, the GNR constructed a terminus under Finsbury Park station that was to be used by the GN&CR trains. The line opened on 14 February 1904 and was taken over by the Metropolitan on 1 July 1913. The line was electrified by the LPTB with conventional Tube stock taking over operation on 15 May 1939 as part of an expanded Northern Line. From 4 October 1964 the service ran solely between Moorgate and Drayton Park, the line north of Drayton Park being utilised for the new Victoria Line (which opened in 1968). The line was closed between Old Street and Moorgate on 7 September 1975 and between Old Street and Drayton Park on 5 October in order to enable the line to be

Above: In April 1933
a northbound GN&CR
service enters the tunnel
to the north of Drayton
Park. In the background
can be seen one of the
GN&CR's old electric
locomotives at the head
of a rake of empty
coaches in the siding.
Note the use of the two
outside conductor rails.
C. C. B. Herbert

Right: Class 313
No 313048 stands at
Moorgate station
awaiting departure with
a service to Welwyn
Garden City on
18 November 1988.
Kevin Lane

incorporated into the GN main-line electrification scheme. EMU operation between Moorgate and Drayton Park commenced on 16 August 1976, although no passengers were carried between Old Street and Moorgate until 8 November 1976, as the escalators at the terminus were unfinished. At the Finsbury Park end a new link was constructed between the ex-GN&CR and the Canonbury curve – thus fulfilling the original scheme of the 1890s – which opened in November

1974. The Moorgate–Drayton Park services were extended to Welwyn Garden City and Hertford North on 8 November 1976, on which date the DMU-operated services over the Canonbury curve from Finsbury Park to Canonbury were withdrawn.

Great Northern & Strand Railway

Incorporated on 1 August 1899, the GN&SR was empowered to construct a Tube from Wood Green to the Strand via Finsbury Park. In 1901 the railway, which despite its name had failed to gain financial backing from the GNR, passed to the control of Yerkes' Underground Group along with the Brompton & Piccadilly Circus, and on 8 August 1902 the two lines were merged as the Great Northern, Brompton & Piccadilly, becoming known as the Piccadilly. The merger was formally recognised by an Act of 18 November 1902. Under the auspices of the Underground Group the extension to the north of Finsbury Park was abandoned, and powers were obtained to construct the link between Holborn and Piccadilly and between Earl's Court and Hammersmith.

Great Northern, Piccadilly & Brompton Railway

Formed by the merger of two parts of the Underground Group – the Brompton & Piccadilly Circus and the Great Northern & Strand railways – the GNP&BR was empowered to construct a line from Finsbury Park to Hammersmith. The Tube line was opened throughout on 15 December 1906. The short branch from Holborn to the Strand (renamed Aldwych after 9 May 1915) was opened on 30 November 1907. The Aldwych branch, always used by a shuttle service, was closed during World War 2, being used as an air-raid shelter before reopening on 1 July 1946. The Aldwych branch closed on 30 September 1994, although both track and station remain *in situ* (and are regularly used for filming purposes if an Underground scene is required).

Left: A three-car rake of 1973 stock is seen at Holborn forming the shuttle to and from Aldwych on 19 July 1988. *Kevin Lane*

Right: Formed of 1973 stock, a Piccadilly Line service stands in Hammersmith en route for Rayners Lane on 21 September 1983.
John Glover

Great Western Railway

One of the best-known of all railway companies, the GWR was incorporated on 31 August 1835 and empowered to build a line from London through to Bristol. Original plans to link with the London & Birmingham at Kensal Green were abandoned in favour of a separate terminus. When the broad-gauge line opened, on 4 June 1838, this was on the site of the future goods depot. The first standard-gauge lines were introduced on 1 October 1851. The new station at Paddington was opened on 16 January 1854 (departures) and 29 May 1854 (arrivals). The final broad-gauge passenger service would depart from Paddington on 20 May 1892. The GWR main line was unaffected by the

Right: Recorded looking towards the west on 16 August 1967, this view shows the GWR main line heading towards Westbourne Park station with the Central Line tracks in the foreground heading eastwards under the main line towards Royal Oak and Paddington. The main-line platforms at Westbourne Park closed in 1992.
British Railways

Grouping in 1923 but passed to British Railways at nationalisation. Since privatisation passenger services have been provided by a number of franchises, the current operator being First Great Western. There is also the Heathrow Express service, which was inaugurated in January 1998 but did not become fully operational until 23 June. This resulted in the installation of 25kV overhead on the ex-GWR main line from Paddington to Airport Junction.

Apart from the main line from Paddington the GWR was also to construct a number of other lines within the area covered by this volume. These include:

Acton Main Line–Acton Wells

This curve linking the GWR main line with the line from Kew to Willesden opened on 1 January 1877. It was built chiefly for freight, but passenger services from Southall to Willesden operated over the line between 1888 and 1912. Still extant, primarily for freight traffic, it is also used occasionally for diverted passenger trains and specials.

Old Oak Common–Northolt Junction

Authorised in 1897, this was part of the GWR's alternative route from London to Birmingham and linked with the Great Western & Great Central Joint north from Northolt Junction to High Wycombe and beyond. The line was used briefly in 1903, but through passenger services did not start until 1 July 1910. The line remains open.

Greenford Loop

This 1½-mile double-track branch with triangular junctions at both north and south ends was also authorised in 1897. It was used initially in 1903, but regular services over the loop were not introduced until 1 May 1904. Passenger services,

Left: The view east towards Paddington station on 16 August 1967, showing the western approaches. Visible behind the bridge that carries Westbourne Terrace over the railway can be seen the goods station built upon the site of the original GWR terminus. The first goods station opened here in 1858 but the building illustrated here dates from work completed in the early 1930s. In 1970 the whole building would be taken over by National Carriers but was to remain rail-served until final closure in December 1975, following which it was to stand empty for a decade until demolition in March 1986.
British Railways

from Westbourne Park to Greenford, were largely operated by auto-trains prior to 'dieselisation' in 1958. The line remains open for passenger services, now provided by First Great Western, between Ealing Broadway and Greenford. The curves at Greenford East–Greenford South junctions and Drayton Green–Hanwell junctions are now freight-only.

Great Western & Brentford Railway

Incorporated on 14 August 1855, this four-mile branch from West Drayton to Brentford was leased by the GWR in 1859 and absorbed formally on 1 January 1872. Originally broad-gauge, the line opened to freight traffic on 18 July 1859 and to passenger services on 1 May 1860. Built as a single track route, the line became mixed-gauge in 1861; the broad gauge was lifted in 1876 when the line was reconstructed as double-track. Freight to Brentford Dock was the line's primary traffic, and the passenger auto-train service – which in April 1910 operated at a half-hourly frequency – was withdrawn on 4 May 1942. Declining freight traffic saw the section between the goods yard and Brentford Dock close completely on 31 December 1964, but the establishment in 1977 of a railhead to handle containerised waste at Brentford has ensued the line's survival.

Great Western & Great Central Joint Committee

Authorised following an Act of 1 August 1899, the GW&GCJC was empowered to construct a line from Northolt Junction, where it was to connect with the planned GWR cut-off route from Old Oak Common and the GC line from Neasden. The line opened from Northolt Junction through to High Wycombe on 2 April 1906. In the 1930s it was proposed that the Central Line be extended parallel to it as far as Denham; in the event World War 2 intervened, and work was delayed. The section through Northolt Junction to West Ruislip was finally opened in 1948. The GW&GC Joint line remains open, the majority of services now being provided by Chiltern Trains.

Left: In September 1954 ex-GWR railcar No 13 stands at the platform of the now closed Uxbridge (High Street) station with a special organised by the London Railway Society. *Ian Allan Library*

Great Western & Uxbridge Railway

This 2½-mile branch from West Drayton was authorised on 16 July 1846 and acquired by the GWR following an Act of 22 July 1847. The broad-gauge branch was opened on 8 December 1856. Originally single track, it was converted to standard gauge in 1871 and doubled in 1880. The terminus was renamed Uxbridge Vine Street in 1907, and there was one intermediate station at Cowley. In April 1910 a single journey over the branch took seven minutes. Passenger services were withdrawn on 10 September 1962, the branch being singled on 18 October. The line was to close completely upon the withdrawal of freight traffic on 13 July 1964.

Hammersmith & City Railway

Authorised on 22 July 1861, this 2½-mile line was opened by the GWR on 13 June 1864 as a double-track mixed-gauge line from Green Lane Junction (Westbourne Park) to Hammersmith. At the time of opening there were two

Left: Viewed from the north on 3 April 1969, a Hammersmith-bound service approaches Shepherd's Bush station. The generously proportioned viaduct visible in the foreground, which straddles the Central Line route to Ruislip and the West London Railway, was built to accommodate broad-gauge track as the line was originally constructed for mixed gauge. The station seen here replaced an earlier structure located slightly to the south in 1914.
Philip Hollingbery

Right: The terminus
of the branch at
Hammersmith viewed
from the south on
19 August 1985 whilst
still branded as part of
the Metropolitan Line;
the line was rebranded
three years later as the
Hammersmith & City .
Kevin Lane

intermediate stations – Notting Hill (later renamed Ladbroke Grove) and Shepherd's Bush. On 1 July 1864 a spur from Latimer Road to connect with the West London line at Uxbridge Road Junction was opened; this was to close in 1940. The H&CR was jointly vested in the GWR and Metropolitan Railway on 15 July 1867 following an Act of 19 June 1865. Following this, the Metropolitan operated the majority of services, the broad-gauge line being removed between Latimer Road and Hammersmith in August 1868 and from Green Lane Junction to Uxbridge Road Junction during March 1869. As a result of population growth, a number of intermediate stations opened: Latimer Road in 1868 and Goldhawk Road in 1914, whilst Shepherd's Bush station was also relocated in 1914. Electric services over the line were introduced on 5 November 1906. The line was taken over by the LPTB on 1 July 1933 as part of the Metropolitan; it was to operate as the Metropolitan until 1988, when a new name – Hammersmith & City – was adopted for the route from Hammersmith to Barking. The line remains open, although it no longer carries freight traffic; this was to cease on 27 July 1960.

Hammersmith Extension Railway

Incorporated on 7 July 1873, the HER was empowered to construct a line from Earl's Court to Hammersmith. The line was opened on 9 September 1874, but further powers to extend westwards were relinquished once the LSWR gave the company running rights over the latter's line to Richmond, the connection between Hammersmith and the LSWR route at Studland Junction being opened on 1 June 1877. The HER was absorbed by the District Railway contemporaneously with the line's opening. The line was electrified on 1 July 1905. Along with the rest of the District Railway the HER passed to the LPTB on 1 July 1933. Still part of the District Line, it remains open.

Hampstead Junction Railway

Authorised on 20 August 1853 and backed by the London & North Western, the HJR was designed to alleviate congestion on the North London Railway. The six-mile line stretched from Camden Town to Old Oak Junction at Willesden. It opened to passenger traffic on 2 January 1860 and to freight on 1 March 1863. Although there was a Working Agreement with the LNWR, which acquired the line on 15 July 1867, services were provided by the NLR. The line lost its freight traffic on 30 September 1972 but remains open for passenger service, currently provided as part of the London Overground network.

Left: Viewed looking towards the east, a Brush Type 4, No D1774, enters Finchley Road & Frognall station with a car train. Work is evidently in hand on the eastbound platform to replace the original awning and buildings with slightly more basic equipment.
Ian Allan Library

Left: Southern Region Class 416/3 No 6325 is seen at Gospel Oak with a service from Broad Street to Richmond on 11 May 1985, two days prior to the final withdrawal of the Class 501 EMUs that had previously operated on the line.
M. E. Haddon

Harrow & Rickmansworth Railway

Authorised originally on 7 August 1874 but abandoned three years later, the line was revived under the auspices of the Metropolitan, new powers being obtained on 6 August 1880. The line opened to Pinner on 25 May 1885 and thence to Rickmansworth on 1 September 1887. It was extended to Chesham on 8 July 1889, and on 1 September 1892 the route from Chalfont Road (now Chalfont & Latimer) to Aylesbury was opened, Chesham being relegated to a branch terminus. The importance of the route was further increased with the opening in 1899 of the Great Central's London Extension, which saw the line north of Canfield Place to South Harrow quadrupled to allow GCR trains to run parallel to the existing Metropolitan lines. The route remains open, the Metropolitan Line, taken over by the LPTB on 1 July 1933, running as far north as Amersham, and services over the erstwhile GCR line being operated by Chiltern Railways.

Right: In July 1952, shortly before the withdrawal of passenger services over the branch, Ivatt 2-6-2T No 41220 is pictured at the terminus – by this date known as Stanmore Village – with a train for Harrow & Wealdstone.
Ian Allan Library

Harrow & Stanmore Railway

Authorised on 25 June 1886 as a two-mile branch to Stanmore, the HSR was opened on 18 December 1890 and was worked from the outset by the LNWR. The line was acquired by the LNWR following an Act of 9 August 1899. In April 1910 a single journey over the branch from Harrow & Wealdstone took five minutes, and the opening of the line encouraged significant residential development in the area. An intermediate station – at Belmont – was opened on 15 September 1932 as suburban traffic increased. However, the extension of the Metropolitan Line to Stanmore adversely affected traffic, and passenger services between Belmont and Stanmore were withdrawn on 15 September 1952. Freight traffic to Stanmore survived until 6 July 1964, the rump of the passenger service, to Belmont, being withdrawn on 5 October.

Harrow & Uxbridge Railway

Incorporated on 6 August 1897, the H&UR was empowered to extend the South Harrow line of the District Railway to Uxbridge. Problems raising the capital required to construct the line resulted in the Metropolitan becoming involved – authorised on 9 August 1899 along with the connection from Rayners Lane to Harrow North Junction – and working the line from its opening to the public on 4 July 1904. The H&UR was formally vested into the Metropolitan on 1 July 1905. The line was initially steam-operated, but electric services from Baker Street commenced on 1 January 1905. The District Railway was granted running powers from South Harrow. District services were replaced by those of the Piccadilly on 4 July 1932, both the Piccadilly and Metropolitan

Left: A service from Baker Street to Uxbridge departs from Hillingdon station, which opened in 1923, on 14 February 1982 formed of A60 stock; the station at Hillingdon was to be relocated slightly to the south in 1992. *Les Bertram*

Left: The original Metropolitan station at Uxbridge was closed in 1938. The replacement structure is seen here in February 1983. *John Glover*

passing to the LPTB on 1 July 1933. The original station at Uxbridge was closed in 1938, a new station opening slightly to the south. Although passenger services, still provided by the Piccadilly and Metropolitan, remain, freight over the line to Uxbridge was withdrawn on 13 July 1964.

Heathrow Express

Construction of this main-line link to Heathrow Airport began in 1993. Promoted and operated by a subsidiary of BAA, the route shared Network Rail lines from Paddington as far as Airport Junction. The construction work was not without controversy, as on 21 October 1994 one of the partially constructed tunnels collapsed, causing a delay to the construction not only of this line but of others in the London area that had adopted similar methods of construction. Services began in January 1998 using 25kV stock, for which the approaches into Paddington had been electrified, to a temporary station, the full service to Heathrow Central and Heathrow Terminal 4 commencing on 23 June. On 27 March 2008 an extension was opened from Heathrow Central to Terminal 5, Express services being replaced by Heathrow Connect on the short branch to Terminal 4.

Above: Heathrow Express Class 332 EMU No 332009 approaches Paddington station on 21 October 2008.
Brian Morrison

Right: Class 332 No 332012 stands at the platform at Heathrow Terminal 5 on 25 October 2008. The line to Terminal 5 opened with the terminal itself in the spring of 2008; the terminal is also served by an extension to the Piccadilly Line.
Brian Morrison

Hounslow & Metropolitan Railway

Incorporated on 26 August 1880, the H&MR was promoted to construct a line from Mill Hill Park (renamed Acton Town from 1 March 1910) to Hounslow Barracks (known as Hounslow West from 1 December 1925). The line as opened on 1 May 1883 saw a slight deviation south of Osterley to serve Hounslow Town. On 21 July 1884 a single-track line from Lampton Junction to Hounslow West was opened; this was to be doubled in the mid-1920s. The line was operated by the District Railway from opening and vested in the DR from 21 July 1903. The section from Lampton Junction to Hounslow Town closed on 1 April 1886 but was reopened in 1903 upon the line's electrification. Also opened in 1903 was a short-lived south-west spur at Hounslow, but this, along with the line from

Left: A Piccadilly Line train approaches Acton Town from the west with a service for Cockfosters. The complex junction here sees the Piccadilly branch towards Heathrow diverge from the District/Piccadilly route towards Ealing Broadway. In the background can be seen Ealing Common depot, which accommodates stock used on both the District and Piccadilly lines. *Richard Lyndsell*

Bottom: Although undated, this photograph of Heston-Hounslow – now Hounslow Central station – predates 1926, when the line was doubled and the signalbox relocated closer to the station, and postdates 1912, when the station was converted into an island platform. The presence in the foreground of what appears to be a discarded 'Heston-Hounslow' nameboard would suggest that the scene dates from 1925, the station being formally renamed on 1 December. *Ian Allan Library*

Lampton Junction to Hounslow Town, was to close on 2 May 1909 upon the opening of Hounslow East station. The line was to become part of the LPTB on 1 July 1933, and the Piccadilly Line took over operation from the District the same year. The line remains open as part of the extended Piccadilly Line, services now operating to and from Heathrow Airport.

London & Birmingham Railway

Authorised on 6 May 1833 between Camden and Birmingham – the extension from Camden to Euston being authorised on 3 July 1835 – the line was opened to Boxmoor on 20 July 1837. Initially, until 1844, trains over the 1-in-77 gradient from Euston to Camden were cable-hauled. The L&BR merged with

Right: A Class 501 EMU forming a Euston–Watford Junction service pauses at the platform serving the New Lines at Willesden Junction on 6 February 1978. The station had been rebuilt in 1894 and further extended on 15 June 1912 with the opening of platforms to serve the New Lines, which also opened on that date north of Willesden to Harrow. Bakerloo Line services reached Willesden on 10 May 1915 and were extended north to Watford Junction on 16 April 1917. *Les Bertram*

Right: The view west along Euston Road prior to the redevelopment and road widening that resulted in the wholesale destruction of the buildings illustrated here. In the centre of the photograph can be seen the famous Doric Arch that dominated the entrance to Euston station. It was the destruction of this structure, along with the threat to neighbouring St Pancras station, that was to prove pivotal in awakening interest in railway architecture in the 1960s. *British Rail*

the Grand Junction and Manchester & Birmingham railways on 16 July 1846 to form the London & North Western. The route from Euston, electrified at 25kV and 750V DC third-rail, now forms the southernmost part of the West Coast main line, and services towards Watford Junction and beyond are currently provided predominantly by Virgin Trains and London Midland.

Left: The view east at Willesden Junction on 29 September 1966, showing the complex layout of the main line into Euston as a northbound block freight, hauled by a BRCW Type 2 diesel and banked by a similar locomotive, crosses on the ex-Midland Railway line from Cricklewood to Acton. *Anthony A. Vickers*

Left: With electrification of the main line to Euston now complete, an 'AL6' (later Class 86) locomotive, No E3169, passes Wembley Central with a Ford car train from Halewood, Merseyside, to Dagenham. *K. A. Porter*

London & Blackwall Railway

Renamed from the Commercial Railway, the London & Blackwall's line from the Minories to Blackwall opened on 6 July 1840 and was initially cable-operated; a second line opened on 3 August 1840. The authorised extension to Fenchurch Street opened on 2 August 1841. On 27 July 1846 an extension to Bow Junction from Stepney was authorised, and before being opened, on 2 July 1849, the original line was converted to standard gauge and prepared for use by steam locomotives. For a period prior to 1 January 1866, when the line was leased to the GER, the route was operated by the LT&SR. A north–east curve, from Salmons Lane Junction to Limehouse Junction, to the east of Stepney, opened in 1880. The London & Blackwall passed to the LNER in 1923; passenger services over the section of the original line from Stepney to Blackwall were withdrawn on 4 May 1926, but, with the exception of its eastern extremity at Blackwall, the line remained open for freight traffic. The section from Stepney to Limehouse Junction closed completely on 14 April 1951, and that from Salmons Lane Junction to Millwall Junction on 5 November 1962. Nowadays the line from Fenchurch Street via Stepney to Gas Factory Junction is used by the successor to the LT&SR – currently the c2c franchise – whilst the section north of Gas Factory Junction to Bow Junction is freight-only. Parallel to the line from Minories is the Docklands Light Railway, which was opened in 1987 and reuses the formation of much of the long-closed route east of Stepney to Blackwall.

London & North Eastern Railway

The LNER inherited all the ex-Great Central, Great Eastern and Great Northern lines in the London area. There was, however, one section to be opened by the LNER, this being the loop serving Wembley Stadium station, which was completed for the Empire Exhibition and opened on 23 April 1923. Passenger services to the station ceased on 1 September 1969, and the station was demolished five years later.

Right: Viewed from the west end of the station, passengers are seen detraining from the single platform at Wembley Stadium station on 24 April 1948. This was the date of the FA Cup Final, a match that saw Manchester United – appearing in the final for the first time in 39 years – defeat Blackpool 4-2. *British Railways*

London & North Western Railway

Formed by the amalgamation on 16 July 1846 of the London & Birmingham, Grand Junction and Manchester & Birmingham railways, the LNWR was to construct a number of additional lines in the London area. These included:

Suburban 'New Lines'

Faced by proposals for an extension to the Tube network from Golders Green to Watford, the LNWR reacted by getting authorisation for the construction of additional capacity parallel to its main line in order to promote the growth of suburban traffic from Willesden to Watford. The line opened from Kensal Green Tunnel to Harrow on 15 June 1912 and thence to Watford Junction on 10 February 1913. The line remains operational, services being provided primarily by London Overground and, south of Harrow & Wealdstone, by the Bakerloo Line. Bakerloo Line services to Watford Junction beyond Stonebridge Park ceased in 1982 but from 1984 were progressively restored to the section between Stonebridge Park and Harrow & Wealdstone.

London & South Western Railway

Although largely to dominate railway development in southwest London, the LSWR built or acquired a number of lines north of the river, in the counties of Middlesex and Surrey. These included:

Windsor, Staines & South Western

Promoted to extend the existing line from Richmond, the WS&SWR was empowered following incorporation on 25 June 1847 to construct two lines: one from Richmond to Windsor via Twickenham, the other a loop from Barnes to a triangular junction between Feltham and Whitton. The first section of line, from Richmond to Datchet, opened on 22 August 1848, whilst the loop line opened from Barnes to Isleworth on 22 August 1849. The loop line was

Left: Formed by Drummond-designed Class H12 LSWR railmotor No 1, a service from Twickenham to Gunnersbury via Brentford departs Hounslow station on 17 September 1910. *Ian Allan Library*

extended from Isleworth to Feltham Junction on 1 February 1850, whilst the triangular junction was completed with the link to Whitton Junction, opened on 1 January 1883. Operated by the LSWR from the outset, electric services commenced over the Hounslow loop on 12 March 1916, those on the main line from Whitton to Windsor following on 6 July 1930. In common with all LSWR-owned lines the WS&SW passed to the Southern Railway in 1923 and ultimately to British Railways (Southern Region) in 1948. Both lines remain operational, passenger services being provided currently by South West Trains.

Right: On 10 September 1966 electro-diesel (later Class 73) No E6014 passes Brentford Central station with a freight from Feltham to Nine Elms.
Brian Stephenson

Below right: Class 421 '4-CIG' No 7356 passes the derelict site of Feltham Yard with the 15.52 service from Waterloo to Reading on 1 September 1979. Feltham Concentration Yard was built in 1917 by German PoWs. With some 25 miles of sidings, it was second-largest in the country and was equipped with two gravity-shunting humps along with repair shops for wagons and locomotives. The yard closed on 6 January 1969. Part of the buildings that survived after closure can be seen in the distance; these were subsequently demolished. Today part of the site has been redeveloped, with the Post Office's Jubilee Sorting Office constructed to the east.
Les Bertram

Kingston branch

Authorised in 1859, the branch from Kingston to Richmond opened on 1 July 1863. Powers to extend the line to New Malden, on the main line from Wimbledon to Woking, were obtained in 1865, and the extension, which necessitated the rebuilding of Kingston station at a higher level, was opened on 1 January 1869. The Kingston loop was electrified from 30 January 1916. The loop passed to the Southern Railway in 1923 and to BR in 1948. Passenger services over the route are currently provided by South West Trains.

Thames Valley

Incorporated in 1862, the Thames Valley was empowered to construct the 6½-mile branch from Strawberry Hill to Shepperton. The line opened throughout on 1 November 1864. The junction at Strawberry Hill became triangular on 1 July 1894 with the opening of the curve from Fulwell to Teddington. The line was operated from the outset by the LSWR and was electrified from 30 January 1916. It passed to the Southern Railway in 1923 and to British Railways (Southern Region) in 1948. Following privatisation services over the branch have been operated by the South West Trains franchise.

Kew East Junction–New Kew Junction / Chiswick Junction (Barnes)– Mortlake Junction

These two curves, linking with the North & South Western Junction Railway, were both opened on 1 January 1863. The latter curve was short-lived, being closed completely on 1 January 1869, but the former was to retain a passenger service until 12 September 1940 and remains open for freight traffic.

Above: On 3 June 1987 an eastbound District Line train departs Gunnersbury station on a service for Upminster. *Kevin Lane*

Above right: A Heathrow-bound Piccadilly Line service formed of 1973 stock passes Ravenscourt Park station non-stop on 18 February 1984. *Kevin Lane*

Gunnersbury–Richmond Junction (Kensington)

This 3¼-mile line was opened throughout on 1 January 1869. Connections were added to the Hammersmith & City Line at Grove Junction (opened on 1 June 1870; closed 1906) and with the District at Studland Road Junction (opened on 1 June 1877). Passenger services between Studland Road Junction and Addison Road were withdrawn on 5 June 1916, the line being abandoned thereafter, but the section from Gunnersbury to Studland Road Junction remained open, trains now provided solely by the District Railway's service to Richmond; this had been electrified from 1 August 1905. Between 1878 and complete closure on 13 September 1965 there was a curve between Acton Lane Junction and Bollo Lane Junction, on the line between Gunnersbury and South Acton, that created a triangular junction at Gunnersbury.

London, Chatham & Dover Railway

Under the Metropolitan Extensions Act 1860 the LCDR was empowered to construct a 4½-mile line from Herne Hill to Farringdon Street to connect with the Metropolitan. The line opened from Herne Hill to Elephant & Castle on 6 October 1862. An extension to a temporary terminus called Blackfriars on the

Left: On 13 September 1982 the abandoned trackbed of the closed line towards Farringdon can be seen as Class 415 4-EPB No 5196 awaits departure from Holborn Viaduct station. Work was shortly to commence on the reopening of the Snow Hill Tunnel and its incorporation into the new Thameslink service. Holborn Viaduct station itself was to close in 1990. *Brian Morrison*

Below right: In 1988 two of the Class 319 EMUs designed for use on the Thameslink service stand at the platforms at Farringdon. Dual-voltage, the EMUs change from third-rail to overhead supply (or vice versa) at Farringdon; south from here the units use the SR 750V DC, but towards the St Pancras line 25kV overhead is used. Evidence of both power supplies can be seen in the photograph. *Alan Mott*

south bank of the river opened on 1 June 1864; this station was subsequently converted into a goods depot. The line was extended across the river to a new terminus at Ludgate Hill on 21 December 1864; the original temporary station built here was replaced by a permanent structure on 1 June 1865. The line was opened throughout to Farringdon on 1 January 1866. The south–east curve at Farringdon opened in 1871; this was to survive until complete closure in 1929. A further Act of 13 July 1871 allowed the LCDR to construct a short branch to serve a new terminus, Holborn Viaduct, which was to open on 2 March 1874, a station on the through line, at Snow Hill, following on 1 August 1874. On 10 May 1886 a second bridge across the river was opened to a new terminus called St Paul's; this was to be renamed Blackfriars in 1937. Passenger services over the line north of Ludgate Hill ceased on 1 June 1916, and the line closed completely on 24 March 1969. However, this line would reopen on 13 May 1985, having been electrified in connection with the Thameslink scheme. Ludgate Hill closed in 1929 and Holborn Viaduct was to follow in 1990, being replaced by a new station – originally called St Paul's Thameslink – on the reopened line to Farringdon. The original 1864 bridge was dismantled in 1985, although its piers remain extant. Today services over the Thameslink route are provided by First Capital Connect, while those into the now-closed terminus at Blackfriars were provided latterley by the South Eastern franchise.

London Docks Company

In 1874 work commenced on the Royal Albert Docks, and in order to serve the new facility the LDC constructed a 1¾-mile branch from Albert Dock Junction to Gallions to serve the hotel and quay, designed to handle liner traffic. The line opened on 3 August 1880 and was intended primarily for passenger and parcels traffic; conventional freight was handled on the quayside lines. Initially passenger services were provided both by the LDC, in the form of a shuttle from Custom House, and the GER, which ran through services, although the latter ultimately took over completely. Passenger services survived until the night of 7/8 September 1940, when bombing by the Luftwaffe resulted in their withdrawal; the line itself was to survive until final closure by the Port of London Authority on 17 April 1966.

London Electric Railway

The Great Northern, Piccadilly & Brompton Railway became the LER on 26 July 1910 following its takeover earlier in the month of the Charing Cross, Euston & Hampstead and Baker Street & Waterloo railways. The company expanded further on 7 August 1912, when it acquired the Edgware & Hampstead Railway. The Bakerloo Line was extended from Paddington to Kilburn Park on 13 January 1915 and thence to Queen's Park – and a connection with the LNWR's 'New Lines' – on 11 February 1915. Bakerloo services were extended to Willesden Junction over the 'New Lines' on 10 May 1915 and to Watford Junction on 16 April 1917. The LER passed to the LPTB on 1 July 1933.

London, Tilbury & Southend Railway

Backed by the London & Blackwall and Eastern Counties railways, the LT&SR was authorised on 17 June 1832 to construct a 36-mile line from Forest Gate, via Tilbury Fort, to Southend. The line was opened from Forest Gate to Tilbury on 13 April 1854, thence to Horndon in late 1854, to Leigh on 1 July 1855 and finally to Southend on 1 March 1856. The line was initially leased for 21 years to contractor Samuel Morton Peto. On the expiry of his lease in 1875, and with the GER no longer interested in taking over the operation of the line, the LT&SR took over operation itself. Following the extension of the District Railway the line from Barking to Bow was quadrupled between 1905 and 1908, and that Barking to Upminster by September 1932. The company remained independent until vested in the Midland Railway following an Act of 7 August 1912, but the MR would not assume full control until 1 October 1920. The

LT&SR would be electrified from the late 1950s, initial peak-hour services commencing on 6 November 1961, and the full schedule on 18 June 1962. Today, passenger services over the LT&SR lines are provided by the c2c franchise.

Among other sections of line opened by the LT&SR were the following:

Barking–Gas Factory Junction

Built to help to develop local traffic and avoid delays at Stratford, this cut-off route was authorised on 7 July 1856 and opened on 31 March 1857. The authorisation included running powers into Fenchurch Street station, which became the terminus for all LT&SR services.

East Ham Loop North Junction–East Ham Loop South Junction

Opened contemporaneously with the Tottenham & Forest Gate Junction Railway on 9 July 1894, this curve was to survive until complete closure on 15 September 1958.

Upminster–Grays

Authorised on 20 August 1883, this line was opened on 1 July 1893. The line was electrified in 1962.

Romford–Upminster

This line was also authorised on 20 August 1883, opening on 7 June 1893. Although threatened with closure it was destined to survive and was finally electrified in 1986.

Below: Recorded from the signalbox to the east of the station on 16 May 1959, this view of the station throat at Fenchurch Street was taken towards the end of steam operation. The newly installed electrification is evident, although it would be a further two years before full electric services were introduced.
Frank Church

Right: Class 302
No 325 recorded on the
viaduct near Shadwell
on 27 September 1983
prior to the
commencement of
construction work on
the Docklands Light
Railway. The DLR was
subsequently to occupy
the southernmost pair
of tracks on the section
of line from just west of
Shadwell to Limehouse.
John Glover

Right: The complex
layout at the western
end of Barking station,
modernised in the early
1960s, is shown to
good effect in this view
of an unidentified
Class 31 heading an
eastbound scrap metal
train towards the
station, modernised in
the early 1960s, on
11 February 1980.
Brian Morrison

Right: Class 302
No 205 approaches
Dagenham Dock on
19 April 1984 on a
service from
Shoeburyness to
Fenchurch Street. In the
background Class 47
No 47014 awaits
departure with a 'Cartic'
train for Wrenthorpe.
Michael J. Collins

Top left: Elm Park was opened by the LMS in 1935 and this view, taken in May of that year, records the early all-welded steel awning that was constructed at the station. *British Rail*

Above: There is one intermediate station on the Romford–Upminster branch – Emerson Park – which is recorded here on 24 January 1971. *J. M. Rickard*

Left: Upminster station was significantly expanded by the LMSR in the early 1930s in connection with the extension of the District Line services to the station. This view, taken on 1 September 1988, shows on the left a service from Tilbury Riverside that has connected with a service from Southend to Fenchurch Street. *Kevin Lane*

London Transport

Until the creation on 1 July 1933 of the London Passenger Transport Board the provision of public transport for the London area had been in the hands of a variety of public bodies – such as London County Council – and private companies – such as the London General Omnibus Co – but the need for better co-ordination and efficiency led to the establishment of a single entity which, under various names, has been central to the development of the capital's railway network ever since. The LPTB was itself superseded by the nationalised London Transport Executive on 1 January 1948. This was to survive until 1963, when it was replaced by the London Transport Board. In 1970 the London Transport Board was itself replaced by the Greater London Council; in 1984, prior to the abolition of the GLC in 1986, control over public transport passed to London Regional Transport, which created subsidiaries (like London Underground Ltd) that facilitated the privatisation of London's bus operators. In 2000, following the creation of the new Greater London Authority, a new organisation – Transport for London – took over the

Right: Work for the extension of the Central Line through to Stratford and onto the ex-GER branches to Epping was approved prior to World War 2 but not completed until the cessation of hostilities. The station at Stratford is served by a short surface section of line and, on 20 March 1982, a White City-bound train, formed of 1962 stock, enters the station from the east.
R. S. Freeman

role of controlling public transport in the metropolis. Over more than 70 years the LPTB and its successors have been involved in a number of projects. Many involved lines belonging to earlier companies and are described in those sections; a number, however, entailed new construction, and these were as follows:

Bakerloo Line

In order to relieve congestion on the Metropolitan Line south of Finchley Road an extension of the Bakerloo Line from Baker Street to Finchley Road was approved as part of the LPTB's New Works Programme. The new section of line was opened on 20 November 1939, on which date the Metropolitan Line's service to Stanmore was incorporated within the Bakerloo Line. The line remained part of the Bakerloo until 1 May 1979, when the Baker Street–Stanmore section became part of the new Jubilee Line.

Right: On 16 September 1978 a Bakerloo Line service, formed of 1972 stock, from Stanmore to Elephant & Castle awaits departure from West Hampstead station. *Brian Morrison*

Central Line

Although there had been earlier proposals it was not until the mid-1930s that plans for the eastern extension of the Central Line were approved, and although work commenced prior to the war the new extensions were not opened until after the cessation of hostilities. The line was extended from Bank to Stratford on 4 December 1946 and thence to Leytonstone on 5 May 1947. The new line from Leytonstone Junction to Newbury Park, and the connection with the ex-GER Fairlop Loop, opened on 14 December 1947. A further extension to the Central Line, this time at its western end, was also proposed in the 1930s. This envisaged laying a further pair of tracks adjacent to the line from North Acton Junction to Denham. As elsewhere, World War 2 delayed the work and the line was not opened to Greenford until 30 June 1947 and thence to West Ruislip on 21 November 1948. The further extension to Denham was not pursued.

Left: A train formed of 1962 stock comes to the surface as it approaches Newbury Park station on the Central Line in 1982. In the centre can be seen the remains of the ex-GER line towards Ilford; closed in 1956.
John Glover

Victoria Line

This was initially proposed as Line C of the London Plan Working Group of 1948, powers for its construction being obtained in 1955, but it was not until August 1962 that funding was guaranteed and work started. The first section of the line, from Walthamstow to Highbury, opened on 1 September 1968, thence to Warren Street following on 3 November 1968 and to Victoria on 7 March 1969. The southward extension to Brixton, authorised by the 1968 Transport Act, opened on 23 July 1971.

Left: A Brixton train arrives at King's Cross/ St Pancras station on the Victoria Line on 29 May 1985. A set of the pictorial tiles, a feature of all of the stations on the line (in this case a cross made out of crowns), is visible on the extreme right.
Colin Boocock

Right: The Piccadilly Line to Heathrow was completed in three stages, the single platform at Terminal 4, seen here, being served by a single-line loop that runs from Hatton Cross to Heathrow Central (now Heathrow Terminals 1, 2, and 3). All trains over the loop operate in a clockwise direction from Hatton Cross. The station and loop opened on 12 April 1986. *London Underground Ltd*

Piccadilly Line

The development of Heathrow as London's main airport resulted in the decision to extend the Piccadilly Line from Hounslow West to the airport. The line opened to Hatton Cross on 19 July 1975 and thence to Heathrow Central on 16 December 1975. The construction and opening of the new Terminal 4 led to a further extension to the line, a single curved loop serving the new terminal opening on 1 April 1986. The latest development, the completion of Terminal 5, resulted is a further extension of the line, a stub to the new terminal opening on 27 March 2008.

Jubilee Line

Another product of the London Plan Working Group, the Jubilee Line was originally proposed as the Fleet Line, the intention being to link the West End with Fenchurch Street via Charing Cross and Fleet Street. Work commenced in 1971, and the line opened from Baker Street to Charing Cross on 30 April 1979, on which date the Bakerloo Line between Baker Street and Stanmore became part of the new line, which in the meantime had been renamed in

Right: On 5 March 1984 a train formed of 1972 Mk II stock awaits departure from Charing Cross with a Jubilee Line service for Stanmore. The short section from Charing Cross to Green Park was closed to normal services following the opening of the Jubilee Line extension to Stratford in 1999. *Colin J. Marsden*

honour of HM Queen Elizabeth's Silver Jubilee in 1977. The proposed extension from Charing Cross to Fenchurch Street was formally abandoned on 31 December 1982. Proposals were, however, made to extend the line from Green Park via Waterloo to Stratford, construction being authorised in 1990. The new extension, which resulted in the closure of the Jubilee Line station at Charing Cross (although it remains intact for emergency use), was opened on 14 September 1999, although some intermediate stations did not open until later in the year.

Metropolitan Railway

Incorporated on 7 August 1854 to succeed the North Metropolitan Railway, the Metropolitan was empowered to construct a line from Paddington eastwards to Farringdon. As a result of the GWR's involvement, the 3½-mile line was constructed to mixed gauge and, following some delays in construction, opened throughout on 10 January 1863. Relations with the GWR proved difficult, and

Left: This scene, recorded at Barbican station on 31 July 1975, features, on the left, a DMU waiting to leave as ECS to Farringdon to form the 18.27 service to Hertford North whilst, on the right, the 18.17 from Moorgate departs for Hatfield. *Kevin Lane*

the latter withdrew from operating the passenger services on 10 August 1863; until the delivery of its own rolling stock the MR used rolling stock from the GNR, which could reach the line via connections installed at King's Cross. The GNR introduced its own service via the link to Farringdon on 1 October 1863. The success of the line prompted expansion, the ¾-mile line to Moorgate (originally Moorgate Street) opening on 23 December 1865, and two extensions – from Paddington to South Kensington and from Moorgate to Minories (Aldgate) – being authorised on 29 July 1864. The line opened from Praed Street Junction to Gloucester Road on 1 October 1868 and thence to an end-on junction with the District Railway at South Kensington on 24 December 1868; the District line opened on the same date. The line was extended from Moorgate to Liverpool Street main-line station on 1 February 1875 (via a curve that was to remain open until 1904) along with a further extension sub-surface to Bishopsgate (now Liverpool Street Underground

Right: King's Cross Midland City station, on the 'Widened Lines', was reopened on 11 July 1983 following the electrification of the suburban line from Moorgate to Luton and Bedford. The station was to close again on 9 December 2007, services being transferred to enhanced facilities at St Pancras, built in connection with the transfer of Eurostar to the modernised and extended main-line station. *British Rail*

Right: On 31 March 1984 a Jubilee Line train formed of 1972 Mk II stock arrives at Stanmore on a service from Charing Cross. The line to Stanmore was served between opening in 1932 and 1939 by Metropolitan Line services, and from then until it became part of the Jubilee Line in 1979 by the Bakerloo. *R. S. Freeman*

station); the extension to Aldgate opened on 18 November 1876. Meanwhile, following authorisation in 1861, the section between King's Cross and Moorgate was widened to four tracks in order to increase capacity. The Widened Lines opened between Farringdon and Barbican on 1 March 1866, between Barbican and Moorgate on 1 July 1866 and between King's Cross and Farringdon on 17 February 1868 (27 January for freight). Passenger services over the Widened Lines from Farringdon to Moorgate were withdrawn by First Capital Connect on 20 March 2009 as a result of work to extend the platforms at Farringdon as part of the Thameslink upgrade project.

The Metropolitan promoted or constructed a number of lines. These included:

Aldgate–Tower of London

Opened on 25 September 1882, this was one of two links – the other being the Metropolitan Inner Circle Completion Railway – that completed the construction of the inner circle.

Wembley Park–Stanmore

Opened on 10 December 1932, this section was to be in the ownership of the MR for a relatively short period prior to the takeover by the LPTB in July 1933. From 20 November 1939 Metropolitan trains were replaced by those of the Bakerloo. The line remained part of the Bakerloo until 30 April 1979, when the section from Baker Street to Stanmore was incorporated within the new Jubilee Line.

Metropolitan District Railway

Incorporated on 29 July 1864, the MDR was normally referred to as the District Railway in order to differentiate it from the earlier Metropolitan, with which the newer railway made an end-on junction east of South Kensington station. The first section of line, from West Brompton to Gloucester Road – then known as Brompton (Gloucester Road) – opened on 12 April 1869, that from Gloucester Road to Blackfriars opening on 1 August 1870, and thence to Mansion House on 3 July 1871. The line was operated initially by the Metropolitan, but this arrangement ceased on 3 July 1871, when the District took over. The same date saw the opening of the branch to Kensington (Addison Road), while the line south from West Brompton was extended to Putney Bridge on 1 March 1880. Following the opening of the LSWR branch from Wimbledon to Putney the District was extended to connect with the LSWR line, crossing the Thames via Fulham Bridge, this extension opening on 3 June 1889. The District was extended from Turnham Green to Ealing on 1 July 1879; between 1 March 1883 and September 1885 District Railway services operated over the GWR main line to Windsor via a connection at Ealing. In 1899 a curve from Acton Town South Junction to the North & South West Junction Railway was completed. Passenger services over the curve, forming part of a service between Hounslow and South Acton, were introduced on 13 June 1905, but with effect from 1 July this would be diverted to Earl's Court. The junction with the NSWJR was severed in 1915, and the spur singled in 1932. From 1905 until complete closure on 28 February 1959 the Acton

Left: An eastbound District Line service, formed of 'D' stock, is recorded entering Gloucester Road station. Gloucester Road was for a period the terminus of the Metropolitan District Railway following its opening from West Brompton on 12 April 1869. *Kevin Lane*

Town–South Acton service was operated by a single-carriage shuttle. The District was electrified from Ealing through to Whitechapel on 1 July 1905. The line passed to the London Passenger Transport Board on 1 July 1933; today the original section from South Kensington to Mansion House sees services operated by both the Circle and District lines.

Right: On 3 December 1982 a District Line train arrives at South Kensington on a service for Upminster. *R. S. Freeman*

Right: In February 1986 a District Line service arrives from the west at Mansion House heading towards Plaistow. Mansion House was the terminus of the original Metropolitan District Railway; the extension to the east was completed by the Metropolitan Inner Circle Completion Railway. *Colin Boocock*

Left: On 8 November 1958, less than a year before final closure, the single-coach shuttle service for South Acton awaits departure from Acton Town station.
H. C. Casserley

Metropolitan & St John's Wood Railway

Incorporated on 29 July 1864, the M&StJWR was empowered to construct a single-track line from Baker Street to Swiss Cottage. Backed by the Metropolitan, it was worked by the larger company from opening on 13 April 1868. The company was empowered to extend west from Swiss Cottage on 5 August 1873, the double-track sections opening to West Hampstead on 30 June 1879 and thence to Willesden Green on 24 November 1879. The 1873 Act also allowed the company to double its original route but this was not completed until 1882. The M&StJWR was formally absorbed by the Metropolitan on 3 July 1882.

Metropolitan Inner Circle Completion Railway

Backed by the Metropolitan and District railways, this was the missing link in the completion of the inner circle – now Circle Line – between Mansion House and Tower of London. Authorised on 7 August 1874, the MICCR passed into the joint ownership of the Metropolitan and District companies following an Act of 11 August 1879. The line opened on 6 October 1884.

Left: In February 1984 a train formed of District Line 'D' stock arrives at Cannon Street with a service for Richmond.
John Glover

Midland Railway

The Midland Railway was created on 10 May 1844 by the merger of three existing railway companies. Initially, following the opening of its line through Bedford to Hitchin in the 1850s, the MR served King's Cross station, but on 22 June 1863 it was authorised to open its own London extension. The line to the MR's own major London terminus at St Pancras (see page 75) and to Somers Town goods yard, located to the west, opened to freight traffic on 9 September 1867 and to passenger services on 13 July 1868. The passenger line remains open, domestic services now being provided by East Midlands Trains. The ex-MR main line was electrified as far north as Bedford in the early 1980s,

Right: One of the main sources of freight traffic over the MR's line south was beer from Burton upon Trent, which was delivered to St Pancras and stored in the undercroft below the main station platforms. Today this scene is radically altered, as the undercroft has been completely transformed to become part of the new St Pancras International station. *British Railways*

Right: Class 45 No 41 (later No 45147) heads the 08.10 Nottingham– St Pancras service through West Hampstead Midland station on 28 September 1974. *Kevin Lane*

Left: Taken from the north, this photograph of Cricklewood station dates from the late 1930s and shows, on the extreme left, the Express Dairy depot, with a Fowler-designed 2-6-2T shunting.
Ian Allan Library

electric services from Moorgate to Luton and Bedford commencing partially on 28 March 1983 after a delay of almost a year caused by dispute over driver-only operation; the full electric service was not introduced until 11 July of the same year. In recent years St Pancras has seen major investment and in late 2007 became the London terminus for Eurostar services, following their transfer from Waterloo International. However, the Somers Town goods yard closed in the late 1960s, and the site has since been redeveloped as the new home of the British Library.

Other lines constructed by the MR included:

Kentish Town–Highgate Road
The MR's link to the Tottenham & Hampstead Junction Railway was opened on 3 January 1870. Passenger services to and from Barking were diverted into Gospel Oak on 5 January 1981, and the curve was to close completely on 11 January 1981.

Carlton Lane Junction–Junction Road Junction
This short line to connect with the T&HJR was opened on 2 April 1883. This line remains open for freight traffic only.

Midland & South West Junction
Authorised on 14 July, the M&SWJR was empowered to construct a 3¾-mile line from Brent Cross Junction to Acton Wells Junction; this line opened to freight traffic on 1 October 1868. On 2 May 1870 a triangular junction was completed at Brent with the opening of the chord from Dudding Hill Junction to Cricklewood Curve Junction. Passenger services over the line from Cricklewood Curve Junction to Acton Wells Junction were introduced on 3 August 1875, shortly after the M&SWJR had been absorbed by the Midland Railway following an Act of 30 July 1874. Passenger services over the route were withdrawn on 1 October 1902, although the line still remains open for freight traffic.

Millwall Extension Railway

Stretching for 1½ miles from Millwall Junction, on the London & Blackwall, to North Greenwich, this was the primary route built to serve part of the rapidly growing London Docks and was authorised by an Act of 19 June 1865. Although the London & Blackwall held the powers, the actual ownership of the line was complex, the railway owning part of it, and other sections belonging to the dock companies along the route; ultimately the route passed to the Port of London Authority. The line opened to freight traffic to and from West India Dock in 1867 and from Millwall Junction to Glengall Road for passenger services on 18 December 1871 and thence to North Greenwich on 29 July 1872 to provide a link to the ferry across the river to Greenwich. Passenger services ceased on 4 May 1926, and the line was closed south of Glengall Road in the 1950s, the section from Millwall Junction to Glengall Road finally closing on 1 May 1970. With the redevelopment of London's Docklands, part of the erstwhile MER alignment was reused in 1987 in the construction of the Docklands Light Railway.

Muswell Hill Railway

Authorised on 13 May 1864, the relatively short Muswell Hill Railway from Park Junction opened on 24 May 1873 contemporaneously with Alexandra Palace. The railway, however, was initially destined to have a relatively short life as services were suspended on 9 June 1873, after the Palace was severely damaged by fire, and not resumed until the Palace reopened on 1 May 1875. Thereafter the Muswell Hill Railway led a somewhat precarious existence until it was taken over by the GNR, which had operated the line from the outset, following an Act of 18 August 1911. The company's name was changed to the Muswell Hill & Palace Railway in September 1886. In the mid-1930s plans were drawn up for the ex-GNR lines in the area to be transferred to the London Passenger Transport Board and electrified as part of an expanded Northern Line. Although some work was completed by 1941, World War 2 intervened; by the cessation of hostilities in 1945 costs had spiralled, and in February 1954 the remaining part of the project was abandoned. Passenger services were withdrawn on 5 July 1954, following which the line from Muswell Hill to Alexandra Palace closed completely; on 14 June 1956 freight was withdrawn from Muswell Hill, whereupon the branch thence to Park Junction also closed.

Right: Photographed in June 1954, shortly before the line's closure, Muswell Hill station was already starting to look forlorn. The line from Highgate to Muswell Hill was to remain open for freight for a further two years, but the extension to Alexandra Palace would close completely upon the withdrawal of passenger services on 5 July 1954. *J. N. Young*

Left: Class N7 0-6-2T No 69694 departs Alexandra Palace station with a push-pull service for Finsbury Park on 2 May 1953.
J. F. Henton

North Metropolitan Railway

Incorporated on 15 August 1853, with powers to construct a 3½-mile line from Paddington to Farringdon Street (now known as Farringdon), the NMR was backed by the GWR and by the City Corporation. In 1854 it was reincorporated as the Metropolitan Railway.

North & South West Junction Railway

The 3¾-mile N&SWJR was authorised on 24 July 1851 to provide a link between the LNWR at Willesden Junction and the LSWR at Old Kew Junction. The line opened to freight traffic on 15 February 1853 and to passengers on 1 August, the

Below: Already overgrown but still six years from complete closure, Hammersmith & Chiswick station is host to ex-LNWR 0-8-0 No 49164 as it departs for Kew Bridge North on 23 September 1959.
Nick Lera

latter service being operated initially by the NLR. The line was leased to the LNWR and LSWR until 1871, when it passed under lease to the LNWR, MR and NLR, but the company remained independent until it was vested in the LMS in 1923. The section from South Acton Junction to Willesden Junction remains open for passenger services, although that from South Acton to Kew lost these on 12 September 1940, excepting a short-lived service, operated post-privatisation by Anglia Trains, that linked Chelmsford with Basingstoke via the Hounslow Loop. The entire route remains open to freight traffic. The only branch constructed by the N&SWJR was the one-mile single-track line from South Acton to Hammersmith & Chiswick. This opened to freight traffic on 1 May 1857, passenger services operating between 8 April 1858 and 1 January 1917. Initially there was simply the branch terminus, but three intermediate stations opened in 1919. The line remained open for freight until 3 May 1965.

North Woolwich Railway

Authorised on 21 July 1845 to construct an extension from Barking Creek, terminus of the Eastern Counties & Thames Junction Railway, the 2¾-mile NWR opened on 14 June 1847. It was bought by the Eastern Counties Railway following an Act of 9 July 1847. G. P. Bidder operated passenger services over the route until 1854, when the North London Railway took over. Passenger services over the section from a point just to the west of Tidal Basin station to Silvertown were withdrawn in 1855 upon the opening of the route via Custom House. Thereafter this section was known as the Silvertown Tramway; this was closed in two stages: the western section was closed in 1967, the remainder following in 1991. However, the bulk of the line was to be reopened on 2 December 2005 as part of the extension of the Docklands Light Railway from Canning Town to King George VI. The section from Silvertown to North Woolwich retained its

Right: It is 13 May 1985 and the first day of electrified services on the North Woolwich branch as '2-EPB' No 6315 arrives at Silvertown with a service towards Woolwich. The unelectrified line adjacent to the EMU was the freight-only single track that ran alongside the passenger line from Custom House to connect with the stub of the Silvertown Tramway. The tramway itself, the course of the original passenger line of 1847, can be seen heading westwards through the closed level crossing. *J. Rickard*

passenger services until 9 December 2006, when the line from Stratford was closed to facilitate expansion of the Docklands Light Railway; on the same date the section from Canning Town to North Woolwich closed completely. There are plans for the conversion of the closed section of line to form part of a new heritage line. The station at North Woolwich was used as a small railway museum from 1984 until closure and dispersal in early 2009.

Above: On 12 November 1960 Class L1 2-6-4T No 67722 is pictured with the 12.10pm service from Stratford to Hertford East. *Leslie Sandler*

Northern & Eastern Railway

Authorised on 4 July 1836 as a 53-mile line from Islington to Cambridge, the first stage in a possible main line from London to York, the 5ft 0in-gauge Northern & Eastern was to suffer slow progress and financial problems, with the result that agreement was made with the Eastern Counties Railway, authorised by an Act of 19 July 1839, to link to the ECR at Stratford and use the ECR's station at Shoreditch. The line opened from Stratford to Broxbourne on 15 September 1840. On 1 January 1844 the ECR took out a 99-year lease on the N&ER, by which date the line had been extended to Bishop's Stortford, and the branch from Broxbourne to Hertford had been opened. The line remains open, services being provided currently by National Express East Anglia.

South Eastern Railway

The SER was authorised on 28 June 1861 to construct a new terminus on the north bank of the river; reached via a triangular junction on the Charing Cross–London Bridge Line, the station – Cannon Street – opened on 1 September 1866. It remains open, services now being provided by the South Eastern franchise.

Tottenham & Forest Gate Junction Railway

Promoted by the MR and LT&SR to provide a connection between their lines, the T&FGJR was incorporated on 4 August 1890 to construct a six-mile line from Woodgrange Park to South Tottenham. An expensive line to construct, the route opened throughout on 9 July 1894. The line remains open, passenger services now provided by the DMUs on the Gospel Oak–Barking operation of London Overground.

Above: Originally known simply as Leytonstone when first opened in 1894, the station was soon renamed with the 'High Road' suffix in order to differentiate it from the earlier GER station. On 29 September 1987 a two-car DMU from Gospel Oak enters the station en route to Barking. *Kevin Lane*

Tottenham & Hampstead Junction Railway

Authorised on 29 July 1862 and with the Great Eastern and Midland railways contributing two-thirds of the capital, the 4¼-mile T&HJR was opened from Tottenham North Junction to Highgate Road on 21 July 1868, the short curve from Tottenham West Junction to Tottenham South Junction following shortly afterwards. From 4 June 1888 the GER operated a passenger service from Gospel Oak; regular services ceased in September 1926, although a limited service on holidays continued until 1939. The section between Junction Road Junction and Gospel Oak was to see passenger services restored in December 1980, when the Barking DMU service was transferred from Kentish Town. When the line was opened there was no physical connection at Gospel Oak between the T&HJR and the North London, but 23 January 1916 saw the establishment of a wartime freight-only link that was to survive until 3 September 1922; reinstated on 11 March 1940, it remains extant for freight only. There were two additional spurs constructed. The first of these – from Harringay Park Junction to Harringay – was started in 1870s but not completed

Left: In 1980 the Barking–Kentish Town DMU service was diverted at its western end to serve Gospel Oak, where a single platform was provided for the service. On 18 October 1986 a two-car DMU, formed of two Class 104 units, awaits departure with a service to Barking.
Michael J. Collins

until World War 1. Restored for use in World War 2, on 8 January 1940, it remained open for freight traffic until 28 April 1968, and from 1983 was used to move HSTs from the Midland main line to Bounds Green depot for servicing. The second spur, opened in 1879, connected South Tottenham with Seven Sisters; this line remains open. The T&HJR passed into the joint ownership of the Midland and Great Eastern railways on 1 July 1902. The bulk of the route remains open, contemporary services forming part of the London Overground network. At Tottenham, the curve from West to North junctions closed completely on 11 June 1961.

Victoria Station & Pimlico Railway

This was authorised on 23 July 1858 to construct a line from Stewarts Lane across the river to a new terminus located on the site of the Grosvenor Canal basin. The London, Brighton & South Coast Railway funded 50% of the work, its half of the station opening on 1 October 1860. The other half, to be used by both the London, Chatham & Dover Railway and the Great Western, was completed on 25 August 1862; prior to that date the LCDR had used a temporary station. Having passed to the Southern Railway in 1923 and thence to British Railways in 1948, the line remains open today, services being operated by the modern-day successors of the LBSCR and LCDR – the Southern and South Eastern franchises respectively.

Waterloo & City Railway

Authorised on 27 July 1893 as an underground link between Waterloo and the City, the Waterloo & City Railway was opened formally on 11 July 1898 and to the public on 8 August 1898. Nicknamed 'The Drain', the line is less than two miles in length and was absorbed by the LSWR following an Act of 20 July 1906, duly passing to the Southern Railway in 1923 and to British Railways (Southern Region) in 1948. Upon the privatisation of British Rail, ownership and operation of the line was transferred to London Underground on 1 April 1994.

Right: The northerly terminus of the Waterloo & City is Bank, where on 13 September 1983 passengers are seen hurrying to join the train during the evening peak. The train is formed of 1940-built stock constructed by the Southern Railway.
John Glover

Below: 'K1' 2-6-0 No 62013 stands at Kensington Olympia station with a cross-London train for the Southern Region on 30 June 1956. The station was renamed from Kensington (Addison Road) in 1946.
E. Wilmshurst

West London Railway

Renamed from the Birmingham, Bristol & Thames Junction Railway on 23 July 1840, the WLR was opened as a 2½-mile mixed-gauge single track from West London Junction at Willesden to the Kensington Canal Basin. The line was unsuccessful initially – passenger services being withdrawn on 30 November 1840 – until the completion of the West London Extension Railway. The WLR was leased by the LNWR and GWR jointly from 31 July 1854 and the line was doubled. At Wormwood Scrubs a level crossing with the GWR main line was

replaced by a bridge in 1860. Although passenger services were once largely unadvertised the line remains open, services today being provided by London Overground and the Southern franchise. In addition to the main line there were a number of connections to adjacent lines. These included a link from Viaduct Junction to Wood Lane Junction, on the Ealing & Shepherd's Bush; this opened in 1917 and was closed completely on 9 March 1964. From Uxbridge Road Junction to Kensington Junction, on the Hammersmith & Chiswick, a connection existed between 1864 and closure to passenger traffic on 20 October 1940. This connection was to close completely on 1 March 1954. At North Pole Junction was a connection between the WLR and the GWR from Paddington; this connection to Old Oak Common East Junction was severed on 29 October 1990, the route from North Pole Junction being incorporated into the access line for the new Eurostar depot. This facility closed in November 2007. At Willesden Junction a connection from Mitre Bridge Junction allowed access to Willesden Junction High Level station and the North London Railway; this opened in 1860 and remains operational to this day.

Above: Hauled by Class 47/4 No 47616 *Y Ddraig Goch / The Red Dragon,* a special from Cambridge running in connection with the Laboratory Exhibition being held at Kensington Olympia passes the weather-beaten and time-worn signalbox at Mitre Bridge Junction on 13 October 1988. *Brian Morrison*

West London Extension Railway

Authorised on 13 August 1859 and opened on 2 March 1863, the WLER was owned jointly by the LNWR, GWR, LBSCR and LSWR and provided a link of just over four miles in length between the West London Railway and Clapham Junction. It was constructed as a mixed-gauge line, but the broad-gauge service operated by the GWR to Victoria ceased in 1866 (albeit continuing as a standard-gauge service until 22 March 1915), and freight traffic to Chelsea Basin four years later; in 1890 the line became standard-gauge only. Timetabled passenger services were withdrawn on 21 October 1940, although

Right: On 27 May 1950 a Clapham Junction–Kensington van train passes the still largely intact station buildings of Chelsea & Fulham station, closed on 21 October 1940. The train is headed by Class M7 0-4-4T No 30038, one of the locomotives painted in malachite green in order to add a splash of colour to Clapham–Waterloo empty-stock workings.
E. R. Wethersett

Right: On 27 May 1950 a Clapham Junction–Kensington van train passes the still largely intact station buildings of Chelsea & Fulham station, closed on 21 October 1940. The train is headed by Class M7 0-4-4T No 30038, one of the locomotives painted in malachite green in order to add a splash of colour to Clapham–Waterloo empty-stock workings.
E. R. Wethersett

a limited non-timetabled peak-hour service from Clapham Junction to Kensington (as Addison Road was known after 19 December 1946) continued. Known as the 'Kenny Belle', this was gradually expanded to run northwards and was later fully timetabled. The passenger service operates today as part of both the London Overground network and the Southern franchise.

Whitechapel & Bow Railway

The constrained nature of the site occupied by Fenchurch Street station mean that it was not possible to expand facilities there, hence the promotion, jointly by the District and LT&S railways, of the W&BR. The 1¾-mile line was authorised on 6 August 1897 and provided a link between the LT&SR at Campbell Road Junction and the District at Whitechapel. The line opened on 2 June 1902, and, although it was jointly owned, all services were operated by the District. The increased traffic prompted the LT&SR to quadruple its line eastwards, from Campbell Road Junction to East Ham in 1905 and thence to Barking in 1908. The LT&SR became part of the Midland Railway in 1912, but the W&BR was to remain nominally independent until nationalisation.

A part from Waterloo and London Bridge, all of the major termini serving London are located north of the river.

Blackfriars was known originally as St Pauls when it opened on 10 May 1886, being renamed on 1 February 1937 to avoid confusion with the new station recently opened on LT's Central Line. The first bridge across the river at this point was opened on 21 December 1864 and served Ludgate Hill station; this station was closed on 3 March 1929. On 10 May 1886 a parallel bridge across the river was opened to serve St Paul's. Blackfriars station suffered considerably during the war but was repaired; it underwent a major reconstruction between 1973 and 1977. In 1985 the original 1864 bridge across the river was dismantled, leaving the newer bridge to carry all traffic. The terminal platforms at the station were closed on 20 March 2009 as a result of work as part of the upgrade scheme for Thameslink.

Broad Street was the terminus of the North London Railway, opening to passengers on 1 November 1865 and to freight on 18 May 1868. The NLR's goods yard was located to the north of the passenger station. The station was constructed with seven platforms, but was later extended to eight. Passenger services over the NLR were converted to electric operation on 1 October 1916. Freight facilities at Broad Street were withdrawn on 27 June 1969 and passenger services reduced to peak hours only in May 1985. Formal closure was approved in June 1985 and demolition started in November of the same year, as part of

Above: The 12.40 Brighton–Bedford service, formed of Class 319 EMU No 319012, makes its scheduled Blackfriars stop on 16 June 1988. On the right Class 415/1 EMU No 5231 and Class 415/6 No 5619 are stabled in the bay platforms awaiting the Monday-morning commuter rush.
Brian Morrison

Left: Recorded on 26 January 1982 as an EMU arrives from Dalston Junction, this view emphasises the close inter-relationship between Broad Street station, on the left, at a slightly higher level, and Liverpool Street, below. Work would soon start on wholesale redevelopment of the area, which initially would entail the reduction of facilities at Broad Street prior to its complete closure and demolition; the campaign, led by the late Sir John Betjeman, to save Liverpool Street station would ultimately prove successful.
Martin Bond

Right: On 11 June 1959 BR Standard Class 4 4-6-0 No 75068 departs from Cannon Street with the last 5.18pm steam service to Dover. The station had received severe damage during World War 2 with the result that, by this date, the original overall roof had been demolished. *J. H. Aston*

the massive Broadgate redevelopment, although final passenger services were not withdrawn until 30 June 1986.

Cannon Street owes its origins to the South Eastern Railway, which opened the station on 1 September 1866. The station was built on a viaduct some 700ft in length; the viaduct required some 27 million bricks for its construction. The station façade was represented by a five-storey hotel designed by E. M. Barry. This was originally known as the City Terminus Hotel but was renamed as the Cannon Street Hotel in 1879. The trainshed was designed by Sir John Hackshaw. Suburban electrification resulted in the wholesale remodelling of track at Cannon Street, the work being undertaken between 5 June and 28 June 1926 and necessitating temporary closure of the station for the duration. The station was severely damaged by wartime bombing; the hotel (which by that time had been converted to offices) was to become disused as a result of Blitz damage in 1941, and the trainshed would also suffer severely, subsequently being demolished.

Charing Cross station also owes its origins to the South Eastern Railway, which promoted a line from London Bridge, via Waterloo, across the river. Work started in 1862 and the first trains operated into the new station on 11 January

Right: The overall roof constructed at Charing Cross in the early 20th century seen here was to be demolished in the mid-1980s to permit the construction of a new office block. Behind the trainshed can be seen the top floors of the Charing Cross Hotel, one of the London hotels then operated by British Transport Hotels and subsequently privatised. *R. C. Riley / Transport Treasury*

1864. The overall trainshed roof was constructed after the original roof, designed by Sir John Hackshaw, collapsed on 5 December 1905. Although the collapse was relatively slow, allowing for the removal of all trains and the evacuation of the station, six people were killed. The 1906 replacement trainshed roof was itself replaced in the late 1980s, when an office complex, Embankment Place, was constructed above the station, but the 250-bed hotel, designed by Edward Middleton Barry and opened on 15 May 1865, remains.

Euston was opened by the London & Birmingham Railway upon completion of the route from Euston Square to Boxmoor on 20 July 1837, services through to Birmingham commencing on 17 September 1838. In both Birmingham and London the railway marked its presence with a triumphal arch. Designed by Philip Hardwick, that at Euston was once described as the 'finest classical monument in London'. The Great Hall and the rest of the building behind the arch, designed by Hardwick's son, were started in 1846, and thereafter the station grew dramatically, such that by the early 1960s it comprised 15 platforms: Nos 1/2 (from 1873), No 3 (the original 1837 arrival platform), Nos 4/5 (of 1891), No 6 (the original 1837 departure platform), Nos 7/8 (short and rarely used), Nos 9/10 (dating from 1840 and used mainly for parcels), No 11 (mainly parcels) and Nos 12-15 (dating from 1892, used for main-line services, and, having a separate entrance, known as the West station). Reconstruction of Euston had originally been proposed before the outbreak of World War 2, but work did not commence until 1963; despite massive protest the famous arch and the rest of the historic station were demolished. The new station was formally opened on 14 October 1968. In late 2007 it was announced that Euston station was to undergo further redevelopment as part of an overall £1,000 million scheme to regenerate the area; costing some £250 million, the work will see the number of platforms at the station increase from the current 18 to 21.

Left: The new station was formally opened by HM The Queen on 14 October 1968, work encompassing a 23-acre site. This photograph, taken from above the Hampstead Road area, shows to good effect the rebuilt terminal and, on the extreme right, the new signalbox and telecommunications centre, both of which were brought into use in 1966. *Taylor Woodrow*

Fenchurch Street — one of the smallest of all London termini – can also claim to be one of the oldest of the city's stations and one with the most complex history. Its origins date back to the London & Blackwall Railway, which company's line from Minories was extended into Fenchurch Street on 2 August 1841. The L&BR was initially cable-operated, a means of propulsion that remained until 1849, when the trains of both the Eastern Counties and North London railways began operating into the station. In order to accommodate the additional traffic the route out to Stepney was widened in 1854, at which time the overall roof – now replaced by platform canopies – was constructed. The next arrival at the station was a company that, ultimately, was to dominate the scene – the London, Tilbury & Southend Railway. In 1865 North London Railway services were diverted to the new station at Broad Street. In the same year the Great Eastern Railway took over the lease of the London & Blackwall; this was followed in 1874 by the opening of Liverpool Street station, which resulted in the majority of GER services' being transferred to the new station. Electric services – initially at 6.75kV – commenced on 6 November 1961, the full timetable being introduced on 18 June 1962.

Above: The rebuilt Fenchurch Street station lacks something of the grandeur of the original. Here, on 21 November 1990, one of the then few remaining blue/grey Class 302 EMUs to remain in service, No 302206, forms the 12.48 to Stanford-le-Hope, despite showing 'Shoeburyness' on the blind. On the right Class 305/2 No 305519 awaits the evening rush-hour. *Brian Morrison*

Holborn Viaduct was the London, Chatham & Dover Railway's second terminus on the north bank of the river and was designed to relieve pressure at Ludgate Hill; it opened on 2 March 1874. On 1 August a second station, Snow Hill, was opened adjacent to Holborn Viaduct on the through lines; renamed in 1912 as Holborn Viaduct (Low Level), it was to lose its passenger services in 1916. Holborn Viaduct was rebuilt between 1960 and 1963 but was to close on 29 January 1990 upon reopening of the line to Farringdon, being replaced by new platforms on the lower level. Nowadays this station is known as City Thameslink.

Right: With construction work continuing on the new office development at the front of the station, this view records the terminal platforms at Holborn Viaduct station in the early 1960s. On the extreme right can be seen the then little-used water tower.
R. J. Marshall

King's Cross was built on the site of a former fever and smallpox hospital, and opened on 14 October 1852. The station was designed by Lewis Cubitt and featured two trainsheds; these were originally constructed with laminated timber ribs, but these were later replaced by iron. The Great Northern Hotel followed in 1854. The station was provided with additional platforms in the 1860s and 1870s, primarily to handle local trains. Always cramped, it was modified in 1972 by the construction of a single-storey extension to the south to house ticket office and retail outlets. In 2005 Network Rail announced a £400 million restoration plan, approved by Camden Council on 9 November 2007, for the thorough restoration of the arched roof of the station and the demolition of the 1972 addition, to be replaced by an open-air plaza. A semi-circular concourse (estimated completion date 2012) will be built in the space directly to the west of the station behind the Great Northern Hotel.

Liverpool Street was opened on 2 February 1874, when suburban trains first started serving the station, the remainder following on 1 November 1875. The station design was the work of Edward Wilson, the GER's engineer. His station saw trackwork modification in 1890 and an eastward extension four years later. Although Liverpool Street was threatened by the Broadgate redevelopment, a campaign led by the late Poet Laureate, Sir John Betjeman, ensured the survival of much of the trainshed.

Above: On 13 May 1966 English Electric-built 'Baby Deltic' No D5907 departs from King's Cross with the 17.41 service to Baldock. *Brian Stephenson*

Left: A Sunday morning at Liverpool Street, 20 July 1949, sees the holiday crowds awaiting departure of trains to the Suffolk and Norfolk coast. In the foreground can be seen an announcement of a half-day excursion train to Great Yarmouth departing from Liverpool Street at 11am on Sundays during August; the price: a princely 15s 3d (47p)! *W. Philip Connolly*

Marylebone was the last of the great London termini to be constructed. The GCR's London Extension was opened to coal traffic on 27 July 1898 and to passenger services on the following 15 March. Adjacent to the station was an

hotel; this was designed by Sir R. W. Edis and opened in 1899. Destined to have a relatively short life as a hotel in railway ownership, being converted to offices in 1945, the building served as the headquarters of British Rail from 1948 until its sale in 1986. Although services into Marylebone were once threatened (and, indeed the facilities were much reduced), such has been the success of the line in recent years that additional platform capacity has been installed to replace that lost during rationalisation.

Above: A Class 115 DMU forming the 09.10 service to Aylesbury prepares to depart Marylebone on 27 March 1984. This side of the station was subsequently to be demolished and redeveloped as rationalisation took effect, but more recently the growth in traffic on Chiltern Trains' services has seen accommodation increased at Marylebone, new platforms being constructed at the station's country end.
Steve Blackman

Paddington was constructed between 1850 and 1854, the original building being the work of Isambard Kingdom Brunel and Matthew Digby Wyatt. As built, to an overall length of 700ft, the station comprised three trainsheds, the central shed spanning 102ft wide, the side sheds 70ft and 68ft. The station was originally provided with 10 platforms – three arrival, two departure and five for carriage storage. The departure side of the new station opened on 16 January 1854, and the arrival platforms on 29 May, which date saw the closure of the original GWR station, on the Bishop's Road site. The new station cost a total of £650,000. A fourth trainshed, located on the north side, was added between 1909 and 1916 and spans 109ft. The station hotel, designed by Philip Charles Hardwick, was not part of the original Brunel scheme but was opened slightly later than the station, on 9 June 1854.

Right: On 5 October 1963 'Castle' 4-6-0 No 7005 Lamphey Castle awaits departure from Paddington with a service towards Oxford and Worcester.
R. A. Panting

Left: Recorded on 8 June 1951, this view of St Pancras shows, on the right, the lines curving away towards Somers Town goods yard — a site now redeveloped for the new British Library — with the great trainshed and hotel of the passenger station visible. With the enlargement of the station and its incorporation within the new St Pancras International this view is today radically altered.
British Railways

Below: Although much of the work at St Pancras International involved the careful restoration of the historic structure, it also involved new construction. This view, recorded on 15 May 2009, shows part of the new buildings, reflecting the prominent tower and spire of the George Gilbert Scott-designed hotel, upon which work was still being undertaken.
Brian Morrison

St Pancras was constructed by the Midland Railway as the terminus of its London Extension; prior to its opening MR services had terminated at King's Cross. The line opened for freight between Bedford and London St Pancras on 8 September 1867 and to passenger services to Moorgate on 13 July 1868, passenger services into St Pancras commencing on 1 October 1868. The trainshed, with its span of 243ft, was designed by William Henry Barlow and R. M. Ordish and was at the time of its construction the world's largest single-span trainshed. The cast-iron support work for the roof was supplied by the Butterley Iron Co in Derbyshire. The roof is tied together by girders in the station floor, which is itself supported by a grid of iron columns; the space thus created under the platforms was used to store one of the most important commodities brought to London by the MR – beer from Burton upon Trent. The 500-bedroom Midland Grand Station hotel beyond, constructed to the design of Sir George Gilbert Scott, was built between 1868 and 1876, although opened in May 1873, in a Gothic style which was to prove highly influential in future railway architecture. After a number of years of decline St Pancras was selected to be the terminus of the new Channel Tunnel Rail Link and has undergone an £800 million refurbishment that has seen a modern extension to the historic trainshed, the opening up of the undercroft and the refurbishment of the long-closed hotel. Standing beneath the roof at the southern end is a statue of Sir John Betjeman; there can be no more appropriate location to mark

the life of this highly popular poet, whose campaigning and influence were central to the survival not just of St Pancras but of other famous stations, notably Liverpool Street.

Victoria dates from the 1850s, when the London, Chatham & Dover and London, Brighton & South Coast railways jointly promoted the Victoria Station & Pimlico Railway, incorporated in 1858. Although the relationship was never wholly harmonious the station grew to become one of the largest serving London. The LBSCR platforms were opened on 1 October 1860; these were used by the LCDR from 3 December 1860 until its own platforms were opened on 25 August 1862. As the GWR had running powers into the station – indeed, was a part-owner until 1932 – some of the LCDR track was dual-gauge in order to accommodate the GWR's broad-gauge trains from Southall. The station was expanded considerably prior to World War 1, the LBSCR section being completed in 1908, and the SECR – as the LCDR had become – in 1909; it was only with the creation of the Southern Railway in 1923 that the division of Victoria into two stations with separate stationmasters ceased. In 1961 Victoria became the terminus for fast services to Gatwick Airport, this traffic being the driving force behind the construction of additional platform capacity in the 1980s and the rafting-over of the ex-LBSCR side of the station.

Below: Victoria station, with the South Eastern section towards the east and the Brighton to the west. Visible in the background are Westminster Cathedral and the Palace of Westminster.
P. Ransome-Wallis

Aldgate A one-road shed, built by the Metropolitan Railway, existed on the west side of the line at the north end of Aldgate station between 18 November 1876 and 1880, when it was demolished. It was replaced by a servicing point that survived until 5 November 1905.

Baker Street Two servicing areas, to the west and to the east of the line and north of the station, were opened by the Metropolitan & St John's Wood Railway on 13 April 1868. Both facilities were closed by the Metropolitan on 1 July 1905.

Bethnal Green (Spitalfields) Located at Spitalfields Coal Depot, just to the west of Bethnal Green station, a one-road brick-built shed was opened by the GER in 1866. The shed closed in 1960 and was demolished.

Bishopsgate Known as Shoreditch until 1846, a facility, about which little is known, was established by the Eastern Counties Railway on 1 July 1840; this was replaced by a one-road shed that survived until closure in 1965.

Blackwall A one-road shed, sited on the south side of the line to the west of Blackwall station, was opened by the London & Blackwall Railway in 1849; it was closed by the GER in 1872 and demolished.

Bounds Green Partly built upon the site of the erstwhile Palace Gates shed, the depot at Bounds Green was commissioned on 1 May 1977 in connection with the introduction of HSTs on the East Coast main line. The main building comprises eight through roads and one terminating line, of which six are for maintenance and servicing, while three form the repair shop. The depot track includes the remains of the link between the ex-GNR Hertford Loop and the ex-GER branch to Palace Gates.

Bow The North London Railway facility at Bow was a six-road brick-built structure located at the junction of the Bromley and Poplar lines. This opened in the early 1850s and was to survive until 1882 when it was incorporated into the adjacent Bow Works. It was to be demolished following the closure of the works.

Broad Street A variety of facilities existed to service locomotives at Broad Street following the line's opening on 1 November 1865. The final facilities were withdrawn upon cessation of steam operation over the line.

Camden The first London & Birmingham Railway shed, located on the north side of the line to the east of Chalk Farm station, opened on 20 June 1837 and closed a decade later. It was replaced by a brick-built circular roundhouse on the same site; this survived in use until 1871 and then reused for commercial purposes. Now a listed structure and recently restored, the building functions today as an art centre. Completed at the same time as the roundhouse (or 'Luggage Engine House') was a brick-built five-road shed, to the east of Chalk Farm station but on the south side of the line. Known as the 'Passenger

Below: Taken from the southeast, this photograph of Camden shed dates from the early post-Nationalisation period and shows the shed as modernised by the LMS in the early 1930s.
British Railways

Engine House', this underwent several modifications before being extended as a seven-road structure in 1932. It closed to steam on 9 September 1963 and completely on 3 January 1966, subsequently being demolished.

Canning Town The Great Eastern Railway established a servicing point on the south side of the Blackwall Pepper Warehouse branch, west of Canning Town station. Opened prior to 1894, it survived until closure in February 1957.

Chingford Located to the north of Chingford station, a servicing area was established by the GER in September 1878; it was to close in November 1960. There was also a second servicing area, to the west of the station; this too closed in November 1960.

Clarence Yard A servicing point was established by the GER on the west side of the line at the north end of Temple Mills Yard in 1883; it was to survive until 1967.

Cricklewood Located to the west of the line and to the north of Cricklewood station, the first phase of the shed, originally known as Childs Hill, was opened by the Midland Railway in 1882. This was a single brick-built roundhouse; in 1893 the shed was extended by the addition of a further single roundhouse. Both sheds were reroofed by BR and were to close on 14 December 1964 to steam; the site was used as a diesel stabling point thereafter until complete closure. The shed has been demolished.

Devons Road Located on the east side of the Poplar line to the east of Bow station, Devons Road No 1 and No 2 sheds were both 10-road brick-built structures opened by the NLR in 1882. No 2 shed was demolished in 1935, the site being used for sidings. No 1 shed was rebuilt by the LMS in 1946 and closed to steam on 25 August 1958, being used thereafter to house diesel locomotives until final closure on 10 February 1964. It has since been demolished.

Devonshire Street Goods Located to the east of Devonshire Street station on the south side of the line, a servicing facility existed here from 1888 until January 1957.

Drayton A temporary wooden-built shed existed between 1837 and 4 June 1838; its location is uncertain.

Edgware A one-road shed was opened by the Edgware, Highgate & London Railway on 27 August 1867; the shed was to close in 1878 and was destroyed during a blizzard in the mid-1980s. With the turntable removed, a servicing point was subsequently established that survived until the early 1960s.

Edgware Road The two-road wooden shed was opened by the Metropolitan Railway on 1 January 1863 on the north side of the line to the east of the station; this was replaced by a stone-built structure on the same site. This replacement structure closed in 1880. Also opened on 1 January 1863 was a brick-built two-road shed to the east of the station on the south side of the line; this closed also in 1880. Further to the east, but again to the south of the line, a further two-road brick shed was constructed for use as a carriage works; this was subsequently used to house locomotives prior to closure in 1880. All the brick-built structures were demolished by the mid-1910s.

Enfield A one-road shed, located to the west of Enfield Town station, was opened by the Eastern Counties Railway on 1 March 1849; it closed in 1866, to be replaced by a new one-road brick-built shed on the same site, opened in 1869. This new building was to survive until closure on 30 November 1960.

Euston station A small servicing facility, of uncertain dates, was sited on the west side of the station.

Farringdon Street A joint Great Western / Metropolitan one-road brick-built shed was opened on the west side of the line to the north of the station on 10 January 1863. It was closed in 1865 and demolished to permit the construction of the line to Moorgate.

Feltham A concrete-built six-road shed was opened in 1922; this structure was located to the east of the station at the western end of the marshalling yard on the south side. The shed was to close on 9 July 1967 and was subsequently demolished.

Fenchurch Street A small servicing facility with turntable was located to the east of the station on the north side of the line. Little further is known other than it opened in 1858 and closed by 1932.

Ferme Park Located to the south of Hornsey station on the west side of the line, a servicing point was established in 1891. Although its turntable was to be removed in 1929, the facility continued in use for a period thereafter.

Finsbury Park When opened in 1960 to replace King's Cross steam shed, Finsbury Park was the first purpose-built main-line diesel depot. It was provided with a single three-road maintenance facility, constructed with a steel frame, brick and glazed side walls and a roof of concrete and asbestos. With the introduction of HSTs and the consequent replacement of the 'Deltic' locomotives the depot was downgraded in importance in June 1981 and would close completely in October 1983. The site was subsequently cleared and used for residential development.

Goodmayes A servicing point, of uncertain dates, was established by the GER on the north of the line to the east of the station; the facility was slight relocated by the LNER. Again the dates of the replacement facility are uncertain.

Hammersmith The first shed to serve Hammersmith was a wooden one-road structure opened by the North & South West Junction Railway on 1 May 1857. Sited to the north of Hammersmith & Chiswick station on the west side of the line, the shed closed in 1880 and was subsequently demolished. The second shed was a two-road brick-built structure located to the east of Hammersmith & Chiswick station and opened by the Hammersmith & Chiswick on 13 June 1864. Used by the GWR, this shed was to close on 5 November 1906.

Harrow-on-the-Hill Opened by the Kingsbury & Harrow Railway on 2 August 1880, this two-road shed was sited to the west of the station on the north side of the line. Closed in 1883, the shed was replaced by a servicing point that survived until 1925. The original shed was re-erected at Neasden.

Hendon A one-road brick-built shed was opened by the Midland Railway in 1870. Sited to the north of the station on the east side of the line, this shed closed in 1882 but was not demolished until 1965.

Holborn Viaduct A one-road brick-built structure was opened by the London, Chatham & Dover Railway on the east side of the station on 2 March 1874. The shed closed in July 1939, although the building survived until demolition in the 1980s.

Holloway A small servicing facility in Holloway Carriage Sidings, located to the south of Holloway station on the west side of the line, was opened by the GNR in 1885. The date of closure is uncertain.

Hornsey The GNR opened a two-road shed on the east side of Hornsey station in August 1850; it closed *c*1866 to be replaced by Wood Green shed and was demolished to permit track widening. A new shed, east of the widened lines at Hornsey station, was opened in 1899 by the GER. The new shed was rebuilt by BR in 1955. Closed to steam in July 1961, it saw a decade's use as a diesel depot. The building remains extant and is currently in use as part of the Hornsey EMU shed. The EMU depot opened in 1976. The six-road shed is capable of accommodating 48 carriages.

Hounslow Between 1850 and 1894 a servicing facility for the LSWR was located on the south side of the line to the west of the station. Between 1 May 1883 and 31 March 1886 there was also a servicing area to the north of Hounslow Town station.

Ilford Opened by the GER in 1901, this three-road brick-built shed was located to the west of Seven Kings station, on the north side of the line. It was closed in May 1939 and demolished. In 1949 a 16-road EMU depot, 656ft in length, was constructed on the north side of the line between Ilford and Seven Kings stations, to serve the new units providing electric services out of Liverpool Street; part of the site was previously occupied by the west–north curve of the ex-GER line to Newbury Park. The depot complex also includes a four-road repair shop and a three-road 'B' shop.

Below: As part of the electrification of the ex-GER main line out of Liverpool Street a new depot was established at Ilford to service the new EMUs. Here, on 13 February 1989, Class 312/0 No 312705 is pictured under overhaul in the 'A' Shop at Ilford depot.
Brian Morrison

Kentish Town No 1 shed was initially opened by the Midland Railway on 8 September 1867; this was formed of two adjoining single roundhouses and was sited on the east of the line to the north of Kentish Town station. The structure was reroofed by BR post-1948. To the north, two further roundhouses – No 2 and No 3 sheds – were opened in 1899; these were also to be reroofed by BR. The shed was closed in 1963, although the buildings remain in alternative commercial use.

King's Cross 'Top Shed', as it was known, was situated alongside King's Cross Goods Depot located to the north of the passenger station on the west side of the line. Initially a 25-road crescent-shaped shed was opened in 1851, but in 1862 eight roads were converted for use as a carriage shed. In the same year a new eight-road facility was opened in front of the original shed; this was modified in 1931 as a through structure to facilitate access to the repair shops in the 1851 original. Also in 1931 seven of the former carriage-shed roads were converted for use by locomotives, this section becoming known as the 'Met Shed'. In 1949 both the original 25-road shed and the eight-road structure of 1862 were re-roofed. The entire facility was closed on 17 June 1963, and the buildings subsequently demolished. Slightly to the north of the main shed a single roundhouse was built in 1859; initially used for carriage repairs, it was subsequently used for locomotives. It was closed in 1931 and demolished.

King's Cross station A three-road brick-built shed, sited on the west side of the line at the north end of the station, was converted from a carriage shed in 1862; the building was closed and demolished in 1873 to facilitate station rebuilding. It was replaced by a new three-road brick-built shed on the west side of the line to the south of the 1862 structure. This was demolished in 1893, although a servicing point was established on the same site until 1924, when it was closed by the LNER, again to facilitate station enlargement. A new servicing point was established to the north of the station on the west side of the line just before Gasworks Tunnels; this was closed to steam in 1965 and converted for use by diesel locomotives. It remained operational until final closure in 1980.

Above: On 23 March 1955 three ex-LMS locomotives – Nos 41724, 40031 and 40160 – are pictured alongside BR Standard 2-6-4T No 80059 around one of the turntables inside Kentish Town shed. *G. Clarke*

Right: One of the most famous locomotives in the world – LNER No 4472 *Flying Scotsman* – is seen alongside 'K2' 2-6-0 No 4659 and 'A1' Pacific No 2555 *Centenary* outside the main running shed at King's Cross in February 1938.
C. C. B. Herbert

Lillie Bridge A four-road shed was opened by the District Railway in 1872 to the north of West Brompton station, on the west side of the line; this was to close in 1902, replaced by a new six-road shed designed to accommodate the new electric rolling stock. It housed rolling stock until 1932, and the site remains in use, now being used by engineering trains. The steam shed was replaced by a two-road wooden structure further to the north; this opened in 1902 and was closed *c*1931. It was itself replaced by a two-road, again located further to the north; closed to steam in 1962, this building remains extant.

Liverpool Street Servicing facilities, including a turntable, were provided at the station from opening on 2 February 1874 and survived until 9 September 1962. Thereafter a diesel facility existed until main-line services from the station were electrified.

London Transport There is a network of depots and sidings serving the various lines of London Underground that serve North London. These are Cockfosters (Piccadilly), Ealing Common (District), Golders Green (Northern), Hainault (Central), Hammersmith (Hammersmith & City / Circle), Highgate Wood (Northern), Neasden (Metropolitan), Northfields (Piccadilly, 1932), Northumberland Park (Victoria, 1968), Queens Park North/South (Bakerloo, 1915), Ruislip (Central), Stonebridge Park (Bakerloo, 9 April 1978), Stratford Market (Jubilee, 1999), Upminster (District, 1958), White City (Central, 2007, replacing an earlier depot). Lillie Bridge depot (1872) is sited to the west of Earl's Court station; this was built originally for Piccadilly and District lines but is now used for engineering stock. There are also two depots serving the Docklands Light Railway: Poplar (1987) and Beckton (1994). Open air storage sidings exist at Arnos Grove (Piccadilly), Barking (District), Edgware (Northern), High Barnet (Northern), Parsons Green (District), South Harrow (District), Stanmore (Jubilee), Triangle (District), Uxbridge (Metropolitan), Wembley Park (Metropolitan) and Woodford (Central).

Mansion House A servicing facility close to the station was opened by the District Railway on 3 July 1871; it closed in the early 1880s.

Marylebone A brick-built single-road shed, opened in 1897, existed in the goods yard; otherwise little is known of this structure, save that it closed in 1914. A servicing point was also established at the station in 1897. This was modified in 1937 with the addition of a mechanical coaler and was to close in 1966. The turntable, however, survived until the 1980s.

Millwall Junction A three-road brick-built shed, located at the west end of Millwall Junction station, on the south side of the line, was originally a GNR goods shed and was converted into a locomotive shed by the GER, opening as such in 1871. Closed in May 1926, it reverted to its former use as goods shed but was subsequently demolished.

Neasden Both the Great Central and Metropolitan had facilities here. The former opened a six-road brick-built shed, sited to the west of Neasden station on the south side of the line, on 15 March 1899; this was to survive until closure by BR on 18 June 1962. The first Metropolitan shed was the reconstruction of a two-road wooden structure erected originally at Harrow; this opened in 1893 and survived until 1898, being replaced by a roundhouse that survived from 1898 until 1909, when it was demolished. Then came a three-road shed, built in corrugated iron, that had previously served as a carriage-cleaning shed. This in turn closed in 1936 and was replaced the following year by a new brick-built two-road structure; closed by LT on 6 June 1971, this last survives in alternative railway use.

North Greenwich A brick-built one-road shed was opened by the Millwall Extension Railway on 29 July 1872. Sited to the east of the station, the shed was closed in 1926.

North Pole This was a purpose-built depot, located on the south side of the Great Western main line, designed to service the Class 373 units used on the Eurostar services from Waterloo to Brussels and Paris. Work on the construction of the depot began in June 1991 and the site was officially opened on 11 November 1992. The depot was closed in November 2007 following the transfer of Eurostar services from Waterloo to St Pancras and the decision that no international presence would be maintained at the former. The site is now awaiting possible redevelopment.

North Woolwich A servicing point, located to the west of the station on the south side of the line, was opened by the North Woolwich Railway on 14 June 1867. The date of closure is unknown.

Old Oak Common Opened on 17 March 1906, Old Oak Common comprised four turntables house in a brick-built structure. The shed was to be demolished in 1964 and closed to steam on 22 March 1965. A diesel depot, which utilised the original steam repair shop allied to a new three-road shed and one of the turntables, was located on the site. Prior to closure this was largely occupied by EWS, and comprised the Lift Shop, the Pullman Car Shed (where the 'Blue Pullman' trains were once maintained) and the former heavy-repair shop known as 'The Factory'. This site, together with the adjacent Coronation Carriage Siding, was acquired for the Crossrail project in 2009 and was vacated by EWS in early 2009. All the surviving Great Western Railway buildings are to be demolished. Adjacent to the Great Western main line is the surviving part of Old Oak Common TMD, the HST depot, where trains operating First Great Western services, the Heathrow Express and Heathrow Connect are maintained.

Osterley A small servicing facility existed to the east of the station; this was opened by the Hounslow & Metropolitan Railway on 21 July 1854 and closed on 13 June 1905.

Paddington A roundhouse, built in timber, with a four-road extension, was opened by the Great Western Railway on 4 June 1838. Sited between Westbourne Bridge and the station, the shed was closed in 1855 to facilitate the extension of the latter.

Palace Gates A two-road brick-built shed was opened by the GER on the east side of the line to the north of Palace Gates station on 7 October 1878. The shed closed in 1954 and was demolished. The site was later used as part of the Bounds Green HST shed.

Park Royal A servicing point, located in the goods yard, was operational between the 1920s and closure in the early 1960s.

Right: Ancient and modern at Plaistow shed in July 1958 in the guise of brand-new Brush Type 2 No D5501 on crew-training duties and ex-LT&SR 4-4-2T No 41948, which was then in store. *P. I. Pator*

Plaistow The LT&SR opened a six-road brick-built shed to the north of Plaistow station in 1896; this was to close in 1911 and was incorporated into Plaistow Works. A new eight-road brick-built shed, sited to the west of the station on the south side of the line, was opened in 1911 to replace the original facility. This shed was to survive until closure in June 1962 and was subsequently demolished.

Poplar A one-road timber shed existed on the north side of Poplar Goods station. Opened in March 1890, little further is known of it.

Poplar (West India Docks) Sited at the west end of Poplar Coal Depot, this single-road facility was designed to house a battery locomotive (MR No 15550, later BR No BEL1).

Praed Street Junction A brick-built two-road shed for the Metropolitan Railway was sited at the junction on the south side of the line; opened on 1 January 1863, it was to close in 1880.

Ranelagh Road A servicing point with turntable located to the south of Royal Oak station was opened by the GWR in 1908. It handled steam until January 1966 and diesel locomotives until the mid-1970s, when the arrival of the HST fleet reduced the number of locomotives handled at Paddington.

Ripple Lane A servicing facility with turntable was established in 1958. Located to the west of Dagenham Dock station, on the south side of the line, the facility was closed in May 1968.

Shoreditch A servicing facility, about which little is known, was established by the Northern & Eastern Railway on 1 July 1840.

Silvertown Goods A servicing area, on the north side of the goods branch to the west of Silvertown station, was opened by the GER; it was to survive until closure on 18 June 1951.

South Acton A two-road brick-built shed was opened by the North London Railway in 1880. Closed in 1916, the structure was to survive until 8 December 1954, when it was destroyed in a storm.

Southall The first shed was a one-road structure opened in July 1859 and situated on the south side of the line to the east of the station. This closed in 1884 and was replaced by a six-road shed sited between the Brentford branch and the main line. In 1922 this shed was modified and in 1943, following wartime damage, the building was rerooffed. This shed was closed in 1953 and replaced by a new eight-road shed immediately to its east. This new shed was to survive until its steam allocation was transferred on 3 January 1966, after which it was used to house DMUs. It was to close finally in 1996 and since then has been used as a preservation centre by the Great Western Railway Preservation Group. Also located at Southall, but on the south side of the Brentford branch, was a one-road shed opened in 1904 to house railmotors. Closed in 1953, it was used to stable DMUs until final closure in 1960.

Left: Photographed looking towards the east, this view records the ex-GWR shed at Southall in the late 1950s. On the extreme right the lines of the branch to Brentford can be seen heading off towards the south, whilst the ex-GWR main line into Paddington can be seen on the extreme left. After closure to steam Southall was used to house DMUs and the building is currently occupied by the Great Western Railway Preservation Group. The Brentford branch, albeit now without its passenger services, remains open for freight traffic.
British Railways

Spitalfields Low Level Also known as Whitechapel Sidings, a servicing area on the east side of the line north of Whitechapel (Low Level) station was opened in the early 1890s; it closed in 1951.

St Pancras There were two servicing facilities at the station. The first was sited to the north of the station, on the east side. This opened on 1 October 1866 and was to survive until the mid-1960s, when a servicing point for diesels was established on the same site. There was also a facility, with turntable, adjacent to the west of the station, in the goods yard.

Stratford The first shed at Stratford was a roundhouse opened by the Northern & Eastern Railway on the east side of the Cambridge line to the north of the station in 1840; this was extended by a four-road brick-built shed running to the north prior to the mid-1860s. The shed complex was closed in 1887 and incorporated into the adjacent works. In 1871 the GER opened a six-road brick-built shed north of the station, to the west of the line to Cambridge; this was known as 'New Shed'. To replace the original shed in 1887 a new 12-road brick-built shed, called Jubilee Shed, was opened to the west of the 1871 structure. The 1887 structure was extended c1900. The building was re-roofed twice, most recently in 1949, before being partially demolished c1960 to allow for the construction of the new diesel depot. Stratford shed was closed to steam in September 1962, and the Jubilee Shed was subsequently demolished; New Shed was retained for a period as a store for preserved steam locomotives. The shed was relocated in 2001 to a new site on the line south of the closed Lea Bridge station, the site of the original facility being redeveloped as the new Stratford International station.

Below: On 16 January 1986 three Class 47s – Nos 47420, 47406 and 47278 – are in the Traction Repair Shop at Stratford receiving treatment for power-unit repairs, a fire alarm earthing fault and collision damage respectively.
Brian Morrison

Stratford Departmental Opened probably in 1930, this two-road corrugated iron shed housed locomotives used within Stratford Works and was to remain open until the withdrawal of Service Locomotive No 33 in December 1963. The building was demolished in the 1980s.

Stratford Market Goods A servicing area, about which little is known, was opened on the west side of the line at the south end of Stratford Market Goods station c1900 by the GER.

Strawberry Hill This shed was known originally as Fulwell Junction, the first incarnation – a six-road structure – opening in 1897. In 1907 it was extended by the addition of a further three roads on the west side. Closed to steam in 1923, it subsequently accommodated EMUs and is still in use today to house part of South West Trains' fleet.

Temple Mills Following the decision to relocate Eurostar services from Waterloo to St Pancras a new depot for servicing the Class 373 units was required to replace the existing facility at North Pole. The new facility at Temple Mills was commissioned on 7 October 2007 in readiness for the transfer of services to St Pancras the following month.

Thames Wharf Yard A servicing facility, about which little is known, was located in the yard to the south of Canning Town station.

Twickenham Opened in June 1850 when the facility was transferred from Richmond, this single-road structure was replaced by a two-road shed on the north side of the line to the east of the original station. This facility opened on 1 July 1863 and closed in 1897; subsequently it has been largely demolished.

Uxbridge A brick-built one-road shed was opened by the GWR adjacent to Vine Street station on 8 December 1856. It closed in December 1897 and was subsequently demolished.

Walthamstow The GER opened a two-road brick-built shed on the west side of the line north of Wood Street station in 1879. In 1898 the shed was extended to the south, doubling its size, and was to survive until closure in 1960 and subsequent demolition.

Westbourne Park A four-road brick-built shed was opened by the GWR in 1855 on the north side of the line to the east of the station. In 1862 a separate three-road brick-built structure was added slightly to the west of the original building; this was doubled in size with a further three-road extension in 1873. The shed at Westbourne Park closed in 1906 upon the opening of Old Oak Common.

Whitechapel A single-road shed, located on the north side of the line at the west end of Whitechapel station, was opened by the Metropolitan in 1882. It closed upon the line's extension to the east on 2 June 1902.

Willesden A 12-road brick-built structure was opened by the LNWR in 1873 on the south side of the line to the west of the station. The building was later extended to the north, but the condition of the roof over this section deteriorated, and the extension was demolished by the LMS in 1939. In October 1929 the LMS had added a single roundhouse, and both this and the original structure of 1873 were to survive until closure on 27 August 1965. Following demolition the site of the shed was used for a container depot. Meanwhile a new depot, designed to handle the new AC electric locomotives that were introduced in the 1960s onwards, was constructed on the north side of the line to the east of Willesden Junction. Capable of accommodating 24 locomotives, this six-road facility remains operational.

Wood Green A two-road brick-built structure, sited to the west of the line north of Hornsey station, was opened by the GNR in 1866. Closed in 1899, it was subsequently demolished.

Given the size of the London area and its importance in the development of the early railway industry, it was inevitable that the area would see a number of locomotive and other works located within its boundaries. The position in London was also complicated by the rise of the Underground network with its own dedicated workshops.

Stratford Works was opened by the Eastern Counties Railway in 1857 and constructed its first locomotives – a batch of six Class A 2-2-2WTs – four years later. Along with the rest of the ECR the works passed to the Great Eastern Railway upon the latter's creation in August 1862. Locomotive production continued thereafter and, in 1891, the works claimed a new record when it completed construction of a Class Y14 0-4-0T in just over nine working hours. Production of locomotives continued through to 1924, when 'N7' 0-6-2T No 999E – now preserved – was completed; in all 1,702 locomotives were built at Stratford. Following the cessation of new construction, work was concentrated on the overhaul of steam locomotives, which continued through to the mid-1950s when diesel maintenance replaced steam. The main works was closed in 1962 on the creation of BR's workshop division, but the running shed continued in use as a diesel repair shed until complete closure on 31 March 1991. Apart from the locomotive works, the ECR also established a carriage works on the site with certain facilities – such as the smithy – being shared with the locomotive works. The carriage works was closed in 1963, work being transferred to Doncaster.

The GER also established a wagon works at Temple Mills in 1896, primarily for the repair of freight stock. The works was to survive until complete closure in 1984.

The North London Railway established its workshops at Bow in 1853. These works were designed to handle both locomotive and wagon repairs initially but in 1860 were extended to permit the construction of new locomotives. The first locomotive to be completed in the new works was a 4-4-0T, No 43. The works constructed new locomotives until 1906, when another 4-4-0T, No 4, was completed. Along with the rest of the NLR, Bow Works passed to the LNWR in 1908 and thereafter handled locomotive repairs. The smallest of the LMS's 15 workshops at Grouping in 1923, the importance of Bow was increased in 1927 when it assumed responsibility for the overhaul of locomotives used on the LT&S section following the closure of the ex-LT&SR Plaistow Works. Suffering damage during the war, the works continued to handle steam locomotive maintenance until the mid-1950s, when it started to handle diesel locomotive work for the adjacent Devons Road shed. Bow Works was finally to close in 1960.

The London, Tilbury & Southend Railway established its own workshops at Plaistow. These were opened in 1880, prior to which date the LT&SR had its locomotives serviced by the ECR and then by the GER. The company acquired all of its locomotives from outside contracts and so Plaistow Works was never involved in the actual construction of new locomotives. The works survived until the Grouping, but was closed to locomotive repairs in 1925 and to carriage and wagon work in the early 1930s.

In 1880 the Metropolitan Railway decided to relocate its workshops from an earlier site at Edgware Road, its original shed to which workshops had been added in 1872/3, to Neasden, the carriage works opening in 1882 and the locomotive works following the next year. A small number of steam locomotives – three 'E'-class 0-4-4Ts – were built by the works. In 1898 a roundhouse to accommodate steam locomotives was constructed; this was to last only a decade, being demolished in 1908. In 1904/5 a 12-road repair shed for electric units was constructed. The depot was further extended in 1932/3 and again in the late 1930s. Neasden remains the primary depot handling Metropolitan Line stock, subsidiary sidings being located at Rickmansworth, Uxbridge and Wembley Park.

The District Railway opened its own works at Acton in 1932, and in 1934 this was expanded to handle the rolling stock from all lines. This function was retained until the mid-1980s, when the decision was taken to decentralise maintenance to individual line depots. The first work to be transferred, in September 1985, involved Northern Line stock, the maintenance of which was transferred to Golders Green depot. As a result of such transfers the workload at Acton was reduced considerably, leaving it to concentrate on the repair and overhaul of components.

Below: A variety of freight stock receives attention in the wagon works at Stratford in April 1975. The works would finally close in 1984. *British Rail*

Although the publication of the Dr Beeching's report on the reshaping of Britain's railways was to have a dramatic impact on the national network, the railways of North London were to escape relatively unscathed. Despite this there were a number of lines and stations that were threatened with closure. These included:

- Broad Street–Richmond
- Harrow & Wealdstone–Belmont
- St Pancras–Barking (local services)
- Romford–Upminster
- West Drayton & Yiewsley–Staines West

The following passenger services were to be modified:

- Euston–Watford Junction
- Broad Street–Watford Junction

Of these lines only two – to Belmont and Staines West – would lose all passenger services in the years immediately following the report, although Broad Street was to close later, the Richmond service being transferred to terminate at North Woolwich (although the bulk of this line is now scheduled to reopen as part of the extended former East London Line).

On 5 March 1983 a Class 501 EMU pauses at South Kenton with an up service from Watford Junction to Euston.
Michael J. Collins

MAPS

Scale 2 inches to the mile

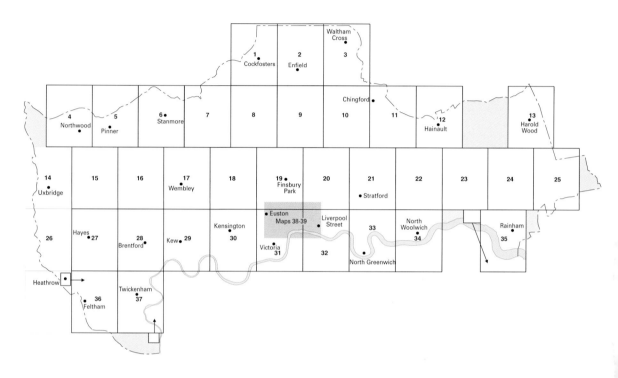

LEGEND							
▬▬▬	Closed line	▬ ▬ ▬	in tunnel	■	Locomotive shed		
▬▬▬	Passenger line	▬ ▬ ▬	in tunnel	**GREAT WESTERN**	Railway company name		
▬▬▬	Underground/DLR line	▬ ▬ ▬	in tunnel	□	Servicing Area		
▬▬▬	Non Passenger line	▬ ▬ ▬	in tunnel	**Abbreviations used on maps**			
PADDINGTON ●	Station open			c.	circa (around)		
(1923)	Date station opened			G	Goods		
Ruislip Gardens ○	Station closed			HL	High Level (station)		
[1964]	Date station closed			LL	Low Level (station)		
1857	Date railway line opened			J	Junction - used with signalbox name		
Clo 1989	Date railway line closed			Junc	Junction - as used in station name		
A4	Main road / road number			Sdg	Siding		
M4	Motorway /motorway junction / motorway number			Std G.	Standard gauge		
level crossing	Level crossing / bridge			Tnl	Tunnel		
⋀⋀⋀⋀	Water Trough			UL	Uncertain location		

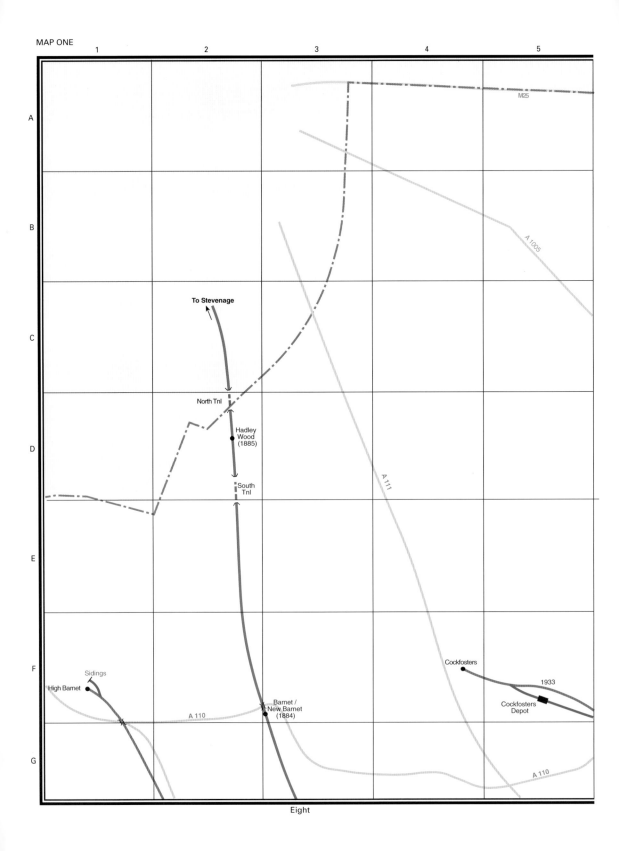

1   2   3   4   5

A

B

A 100S

M25

To Stevenage

C

North Tnl

Hadley
Wood
(1885)

D

A 111

South
Tnl

E

F

Cockfosters

Sidings

1933

High Barnet

Cockfosters
Depot

Barnet /
New Barnet
(1884)

A 110

G

A 110

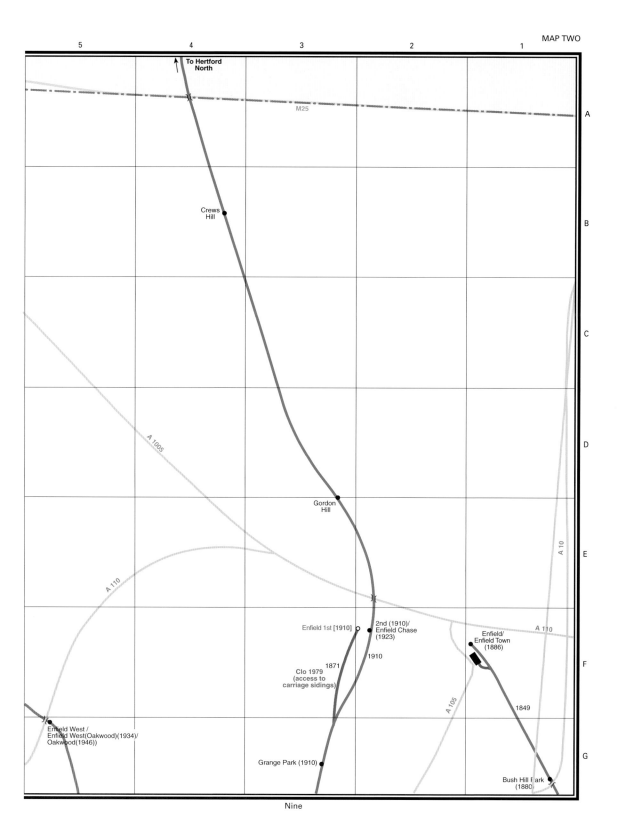

5   4   3   2   1

To Hertford North

M25

A

Crews Hill

B

C

A 1005

D

Gordon Hill

A 10

E

A 110

Enfield 1st [1910]

2nd (1910)/ Enfield Chase (1923)

Enfield/ Enfield Town (1886)

A 110

1910

1871

Clo 1979 (access to carriage sidings)

A 105

F

Enfield West / Enfield West(Oakwood)(1934)/ Oakwood(1946))

1849

Grange Park (1910)

Bush Hill Park (1880)

G

Nine

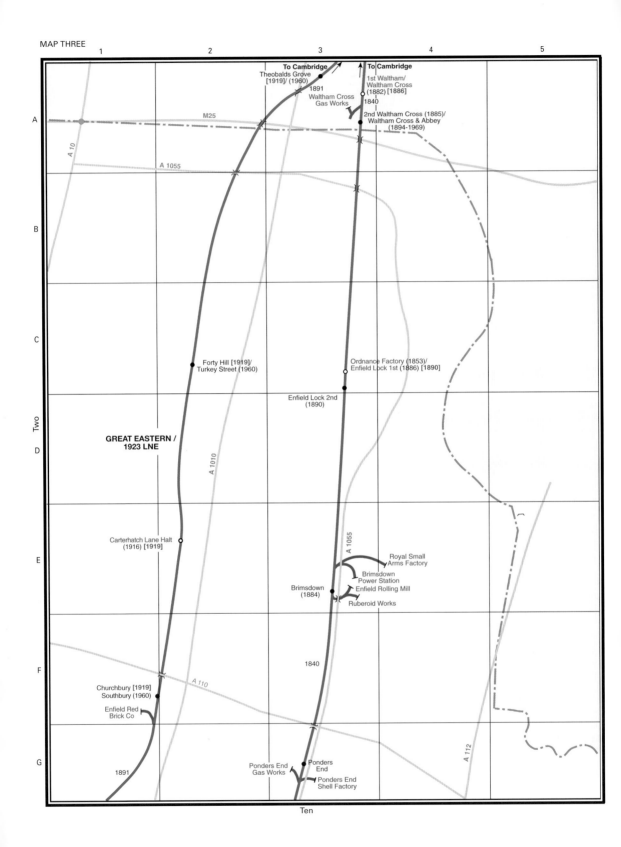

1   2   3   4   5

To Cambridge
Theobalds Grove
[1919]/ (1960)
1891
Waltham Cross
Gas Works

To Cambridge
1st Waltham/
Waltham Cross
(1882) [1886]
1840

2nd Waltham Cross (1885)/
Waltham Cross & Abbey
(1894-1969)

A

M25

A 10

A 1055

B

C

Forty Hill [1919]/
Turkey Street (1960)

Ordnance Factory (1853)/
Enfield Lock 1st (1886) [1890]

Enfield Lock 2nd
(1890)

Two

**GREAT EASTERN /
1923 LNE**

D

A 1010

Carterhatch Lane Halt
(1916) [1919]

A 1055

Royal Small
Arms Factory

E

Brimsdown
Power Station
Enfield Rolling Mill

Brimsdown
(1884)

Ruberoid Works

1840

F

Churchbury [1919]
Southbury (1960)

A 110

Enfield Red
Brick Co

A 112

G

1891

Ponders End
Gas Works

Ponders
End

Ponders End
Shell Factory

Ten

5   4   3   2   1

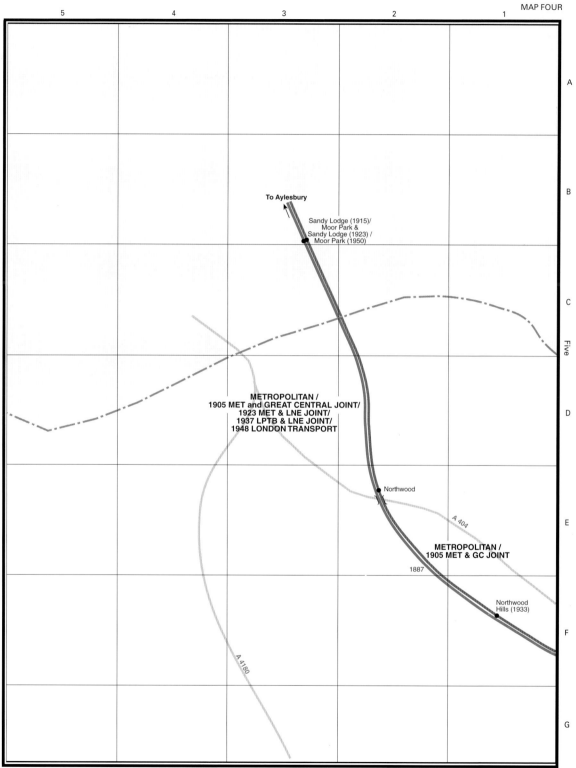

To Aylesbury

Sandy Lodge (1915)/
Moor Park &
Sandy Lodge (1923) /
Moor Park (1950)

**METROPOLITAN /
1905 MET and GREAT CENTRAL JOINT/
1923 MET & LNE JOINT/
1937 LPTB & LNE JOINT/
1948 LONDON TRANSPORT**

Northwood

A 404

**METROPOLITAN /
1905 MET & GC JOINT**

1887

Northwood
Hills (1933)

A 4180

Five

A

B

C

D

E

F

G

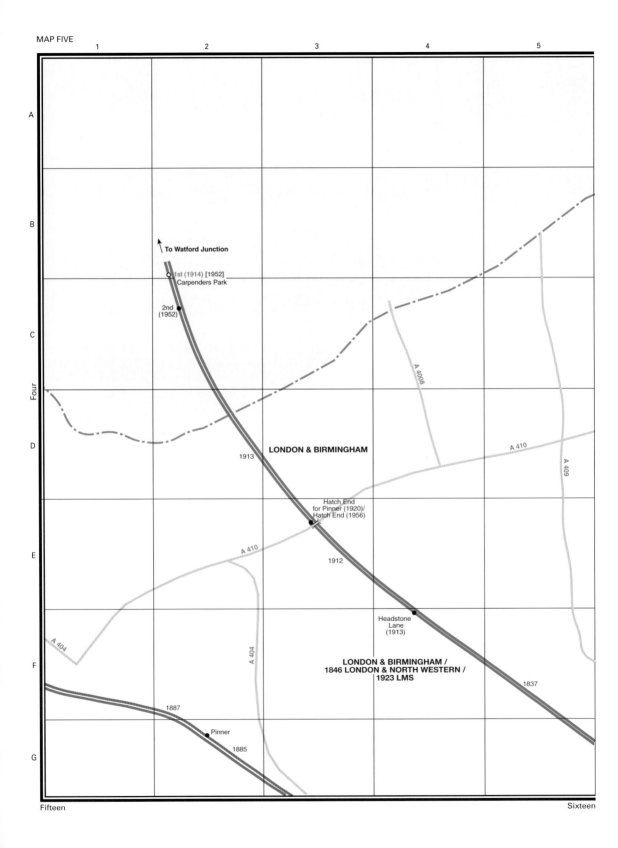

1   2   3   4   5

A

B

To Watford Junction

1st (1914) [1952]
Carpenders Park

2nd
(1952)

C

A 4008

Four

D

1913   LONDON & BIRMINGHAM   A 410   A 409

Hatch End
for Pinner (1920)/
Hatch End (1956)

A 410

E   1912

Headstone
Lane
(1913)

A 404

A 404   LONDON & BIRMINGHAM /
F   1846 LONDON & NORTH WESTERN /   1837
1923 LMS

1887

Pinner

G   1885

5   4   3   2   1

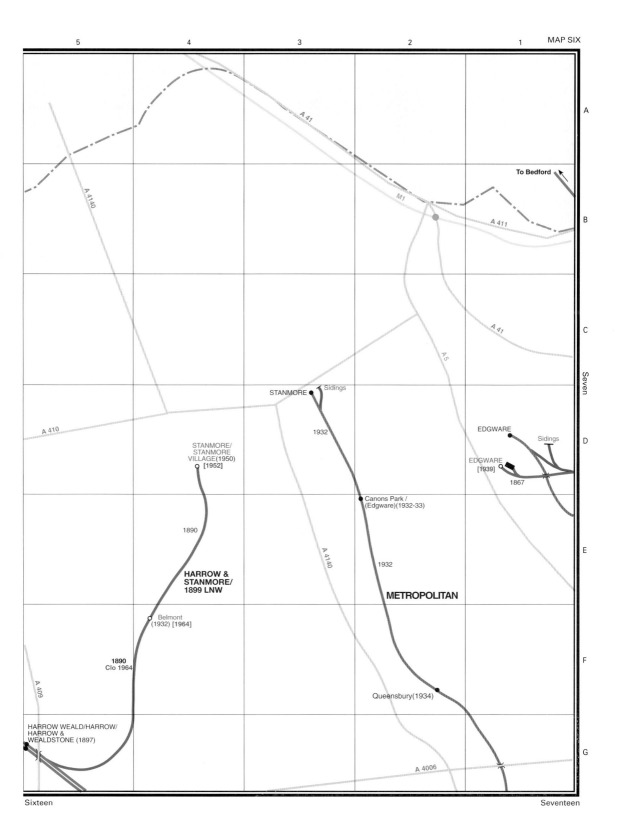

A
A 41

To Bedford

M1

B
A 411

C
A 41

A 5

Seven

STANMORE ● ← Sidings

1932

EDGWARE
●
Sidings

D
A 410

STANMORE/
STANMORE
VILLAGE(1950)
○ [1952]

EDGWARE
[1939] ○

1867

● Canons Park /
(Edgware)(1932-33)

1890

E

HARROW &
STANMORE/
1899 LNW

1932

METROPOLITAN

○ Belmont
(1932) [1964]

1890
Clo 1964

F
A 409

Queensbury(1934) ●

HARROW WEALD/HARROW/
HARROW &
WEALDSTONE (1897)

G

A 4006

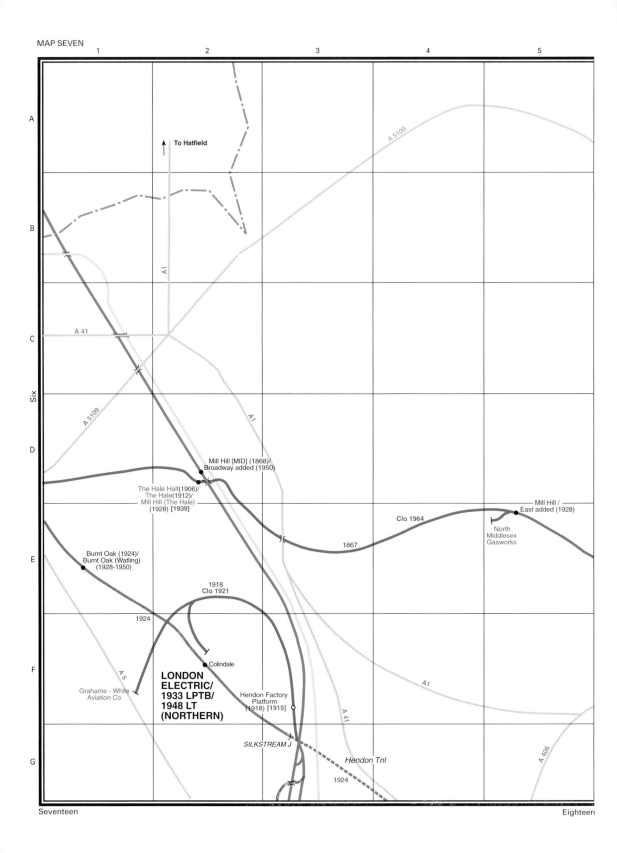

↑ To Hatfield

A1

A 41

A 5109

A 5109

A1

Mill Hill [MID] (1868)/
Broadway added (1950)

The Hale Halt(1906)/
The Hale(1912)/
Mill Hill (The Hale)
(1928) [1939]

Mill Hill /
East added (1928)

Clo 1964

North
Middlesex
Gasworks

Burnt Oak (1924)/
Burnt Oak (Watling)
(1928-1950)

1867

1918
Clo 1921

1924

A 5

Colindale

LONDON
ELECTRIC/
1933 LPTB/
1948 LT
(NORTHERN)

Grahame - White
Aviation Co

Hendon Factory
Platform
(1918) [1919]

A1

A 41

SILKSTREAM J

Hendon Tnl

A 406

1924

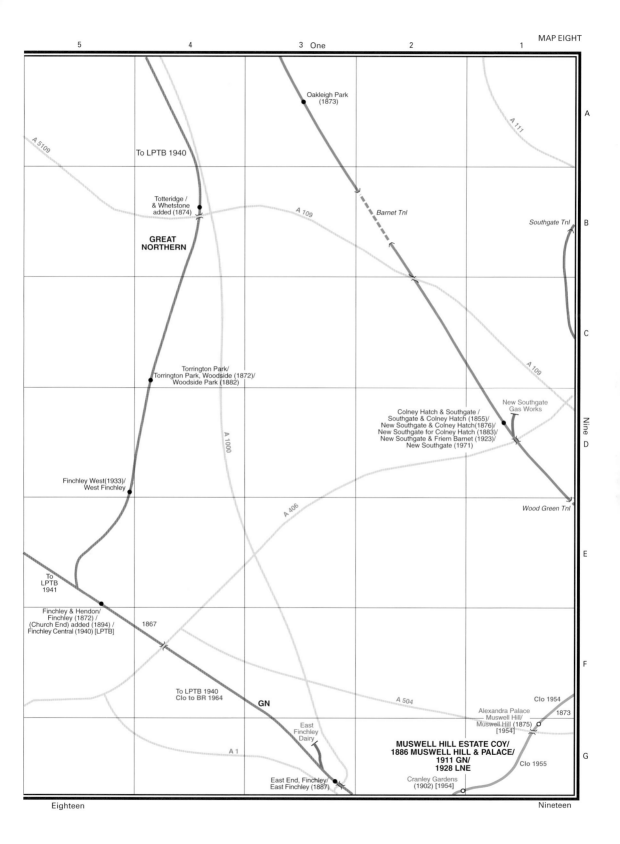

5   4   3 One   2   1

A 111

A

To LPTB 1940

A 5109

Oakleigh Park
(1873)

Totteridge /
& Whetstone
added (1874)

A 109

Barnet Tnl

Southgate Tnl

B

**GREAT
NORTHERN**

C

Torrington Park/
Torrington Park, Woodside (1872)/
Woodside Park (1882)

A 109

New Southgate
Gas Works

Colney Hatch & Southgate /
Southgate & Colney Hatch (1855)/
New Southgate & Colney Hatch (1876)/
New Southgate for Colney Hatch (1883)/
New Southgate & Friern Barnet (1923)/
New Southgate (1971)

A 1000

Nine

D

Finchley West(1933)/
West Finchley

A 406

Wood Green Tnl

E

To
LPTB
1941

Finchley & Hendon/
Finchley (1872) /
(Church End) added (1894) /
Finchley Central (1940) [LPTB]

1867

F

To LPTB 1940
Clo to BR 1964

GN

A 504

Clo 1954

1873

Alexandra Palace
Muswell Hill/
Muswell Hill (1875)
[1954]

East
Finchley
Dairy

A 1

**MUSWELL HILL ESTATE COY/
1886 MUSWELL HILL & PALACE/
1911 GN/
1928 LNE**

Clo 1955

G

East End, Finchley/
East Finchley (1887)

Cranley Gardens
(1902) [1954]

Eighteen

Nineteen

MAP NINE

1
2
3
Two
4
5
A
B
C
D
E
F
G
Nine
Nineteen
Twenty
EASTERN COUNTIES / 1862 GREAT EASTERN / 1923 LNE
Winchmore Hill
Southgate
Southgate Tnl
A 111
A 10
A 105
Palmers Green/ Palmers Green & Southgate (1876-1971)
1933
Arnos Grove 1932
Siding
A 110
1871
A 406
GREAT EASTERN
Bounds Green
Bowes Park (1880)
Wood Green Tnl
A 1010
White Hart Lane
1929
Clo 1964
LNE
A 10
Palace Gates, Wood Green [1963]
Bounds Green Depot
Wood Green (1859)/ Woods Green (Alexandra Palace)(1864-1871)/ Alexandra Palace (second) (1982)
Wood Green
A 109
GE
1878
Green Lanes/Green Lanes & Noel Park (1884)/ Noel Park & Wood Green(1902)[1963]
1850
ALEXANDRA PALACE(first)/ Alexandra Park (1891-92) [1954]
Bruce Grove
GE
A 1080
Metropolitan Water Board's Siding
A 10
A 504
West Green [1963]
A 504
1872
GREAT NORTHERN / 1923 LNE
Hornsey
Clo 1964 1878

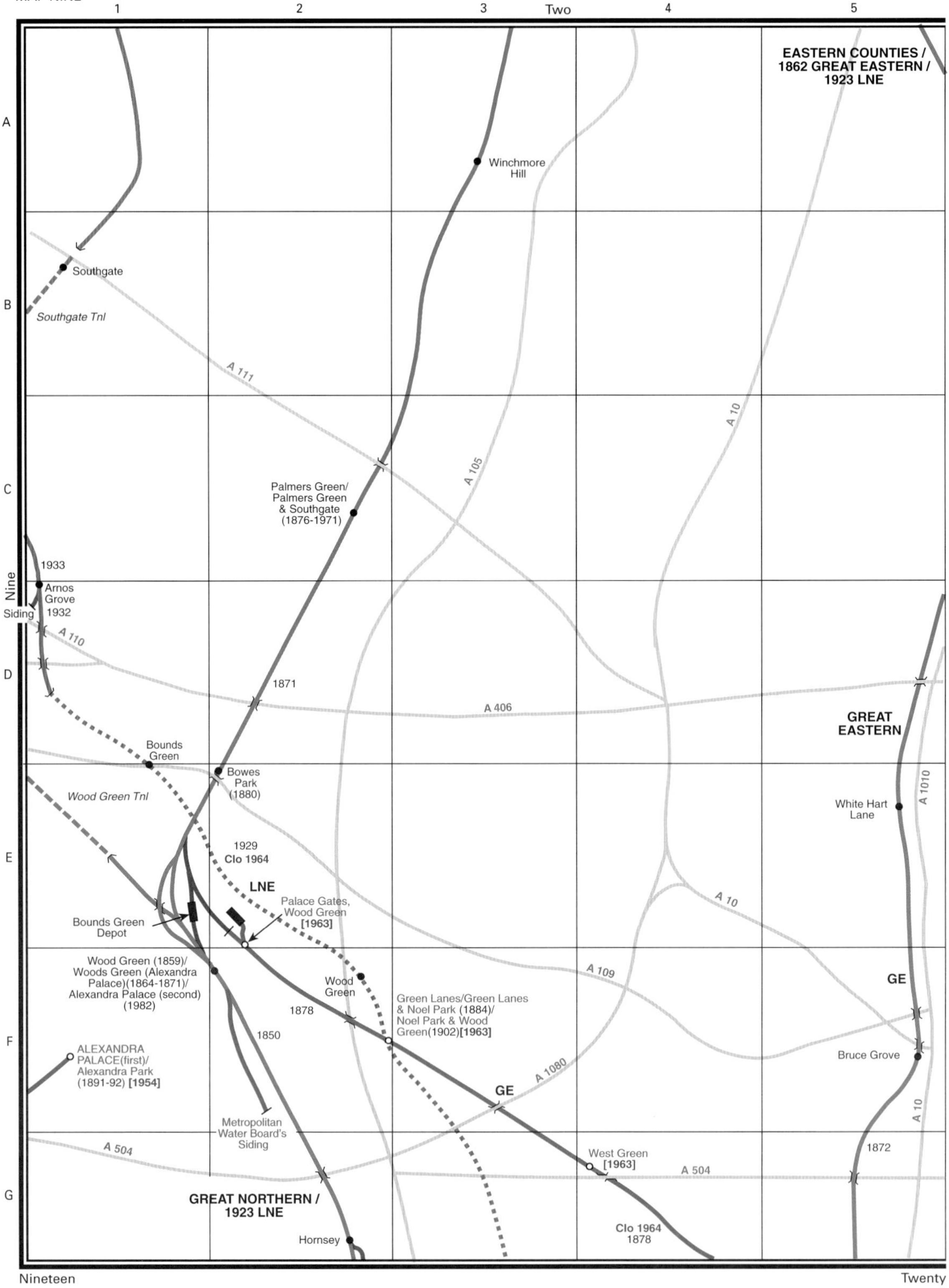

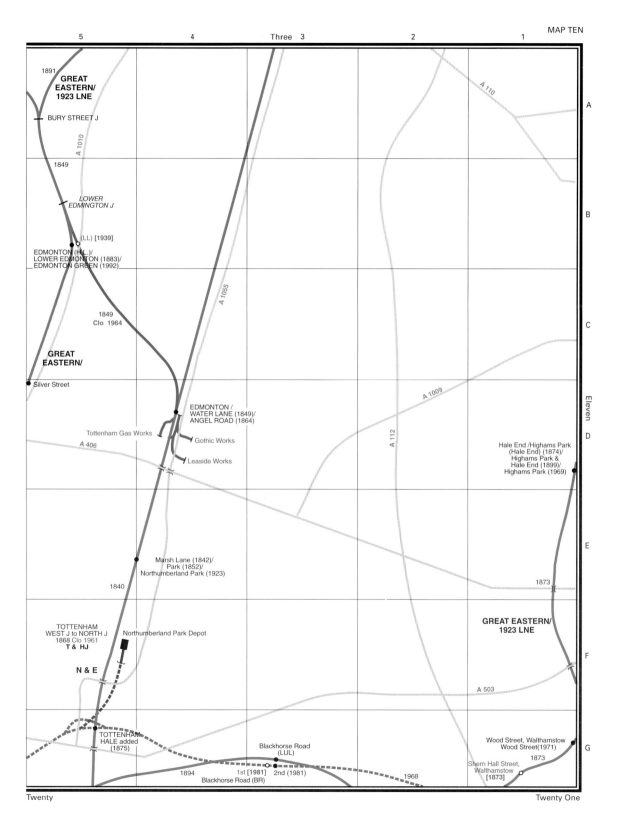

5   4   Three   3   2   1

A 110

1891

GREAT EASTERN/ 1923 LNE

A

— BURY STREET J

A 1010

1849

B

LOWER EDMINGTON J

(LL) [1939]

EDMONTON (H.L.)/
LOWER EDMONTON (1883)/
EDMONTON GREEN (1992)

A 1055

1849
Clo 1964

C

GREAT EASTERN/

A 1009

Eleven

Silver Street

EDMONTON /
WATER LANE (1849)/
ANGEL ROAD (1864)

A 112

Tottenham Gas Works

Gothic Works

D

A 406

Leaside Works

Hale End /Highams Park
(Hale End) (1874)/
Highams Park &
Hale End (1899)/
Highams Park (1969)

E

Marsh Lane (1842)/
Park (1852)/
Northumberland Park (1923)

1840

1873

**GREAT EASTERN/
1923 LNE**

TOTTENHAM
WEST J to NORTH J
1868 Clo 1961
T & HJ

Northumberland Park Depot

F

A 503

N & E

TOTTENHAM
HALE added
(1875)

Blackhorse Road
(LUL)

Wood Street, Walthamstow
Wood Street(1971)

G

1894   1st [1981]   2nd (1981)
Blackhorse Road (BR)

1968

1873

Shern Hall Street,
Walthamstow
[1873]

1   2   3   4   5

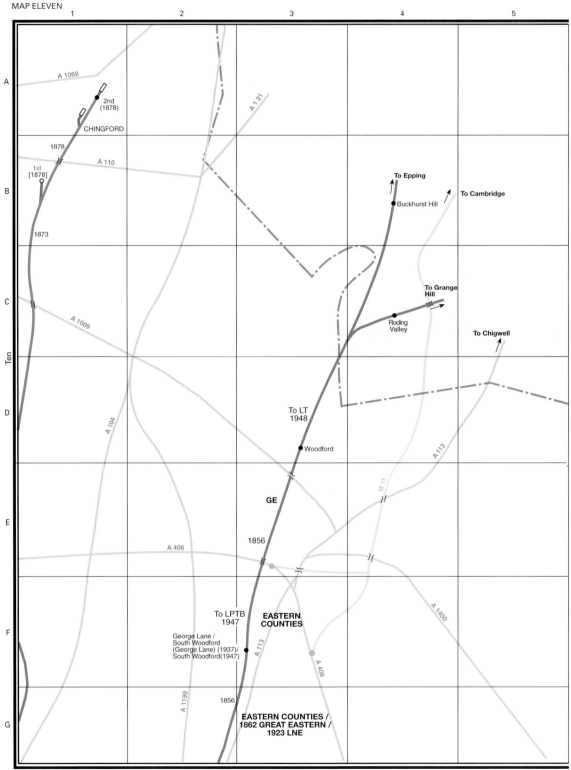

A

A 1069

2nd
(1878)

CHINGFORD

A 121

1878

A 110

1st
[1878]

B

To Epping

To Cambridge

Buckhurst Hill

1873

To Grange
Hill

C

A 1009

To Chigwell

Roding
Valley

Ten

D

A 104

To LT
1948

A 113

Woodford

GE

E

A 406

1856

M 11

To LPTB
1947

EASTERN
COUNTIES

F

George Lane /
South Woodford
(George Lane) (1937)/
South Woodford(1947)

A 113

A 1400

A 406

A 1199

1856

EASTERN COUNTIES /
1862 GREAT EASTERN /
1923 LNE

G

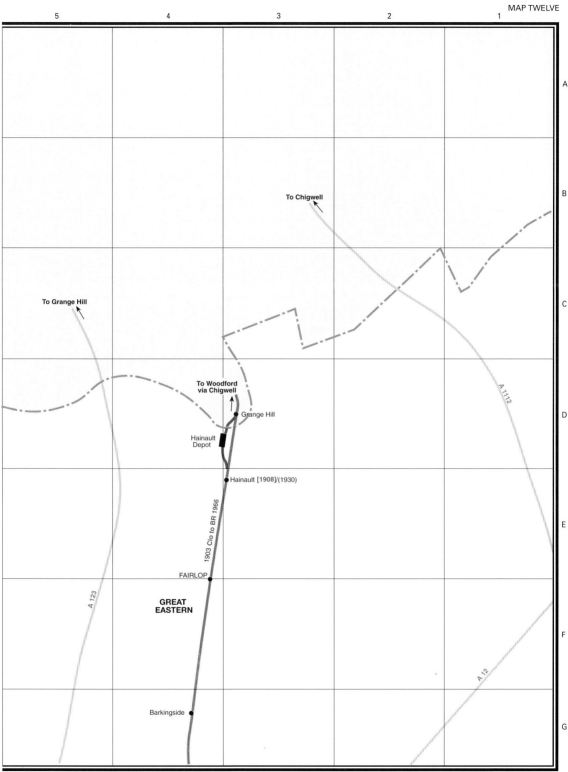

5   4   3   2   1

A

To Chigwell   B

To Grange Hill   C

**To Woodford
via Chigwell**

Grange Hill   D

Hainault
Depot

Hainault [1908]/(1930)

A 1112

1903 Clo to BR 1966

E

FAIRLOP

**GREAT
EASTERN**

A 123

A 12

F

Barkingside

G

1 2 3 4 5

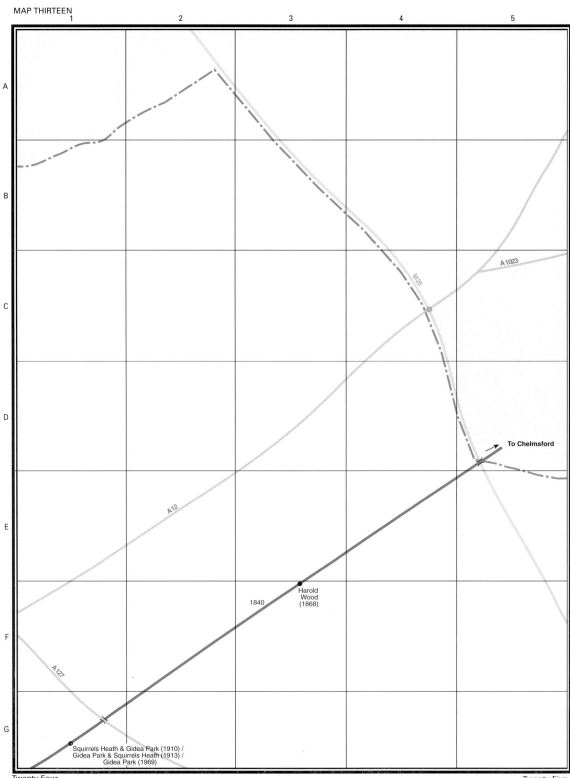

A

B

C

A 1023

M25

D

To Chelmsford

A12

E

Harold
Wood
(1868)

1840

F

A 127

G

Squirrels Heath & Gidea Park (1910) /
Gidea Park & Squirrels Heath (1913) /
Gidea Park (1969)

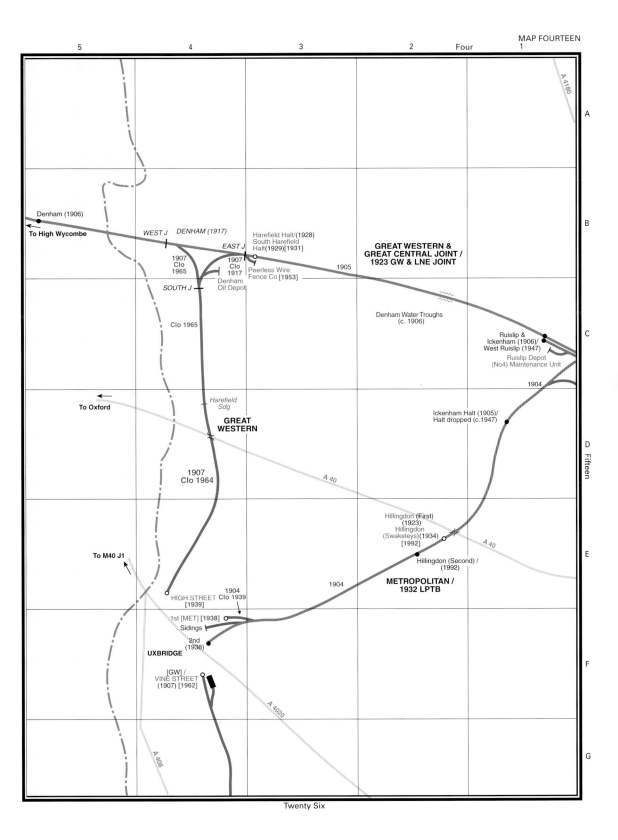

5 4 3 2 Four 1

A

A 4180

Denham (1906)
To High Wycombe

WEST J DENHAM (1917)

EAST J

B

Harefield Halt/(1928)
South Harefield
Halt(1929)[1931]

GREAT WESTERN &
GREAT CENTRAL JOINT /
1923 GW & LNE JOINT

1907
Clo
1965

1907
Clo
1917

Peerless Wire
Fence Co [1953]

1905

SOUTH J

Denham
Oil Depot

Denham Water Troughs
(c. 1906)

Clo 1965

C

Ruislip &
Ickenham (1906)/
West Ruislip (1947)

Ruislip Depot
(No4) Maintenance Unit

To Oxford

Harefield
Sdg

GREAT
WESTERN

1904

Ickenham Halt (1905)/
Halt dropped (c.1947)

D

Fifteen

1907
Clo 1964

A 40

Hillingdon (First)
(1923)
Hillingdon
(Swakeleys)(1934)
[1992]

A 40

E

To M40 J1

Hillingdon (Second) /
(1992)

METROPOLITAN /
1932 LPTB

1904

1904

HIGH STREET
[1939]

Clo 1939

1st [MET] [1938]

Sidings

2nd
(1938)

UXBRIDGE

F

[GW] /
VINE STREET
(1907) [1962]

A 4020

G

A 408

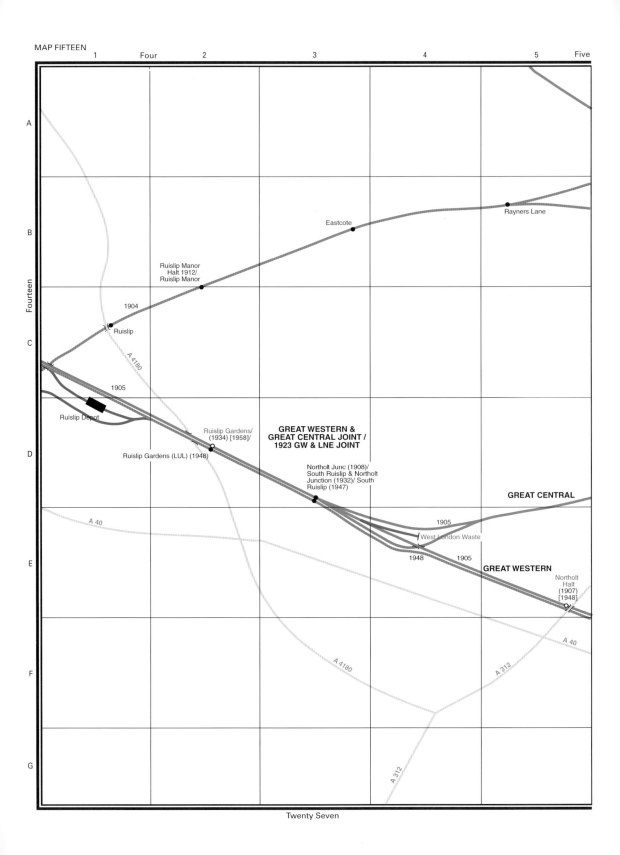

A

B

Fourteen

Eastcote

Rayners Lane

Ruislip Manor
Halt 1912/
Ruislip Manor

1904

C

Ruislip

A 4180

1905

Ruislip Depot

D

Ruislip Gardens/
(1934) [1958]/

Ruislip Gardens (LUL) (1948)

**GREAT WESTERN &
GREAT CENTRAL JOINT /
1923 GW & LNE JOINT**

Northolt Junc (1908)/
South Ruislip & Northolt
Junction (1932)/ South
Ruislip (1947)

GREAT CENTRAL

A 40

1905

West London Waste

1948   1905

GREAT WESTERN

E

Northolt
Halt
(1907)
[1948]

A 40

A 312

F

A 4180

A 312

G

A 312

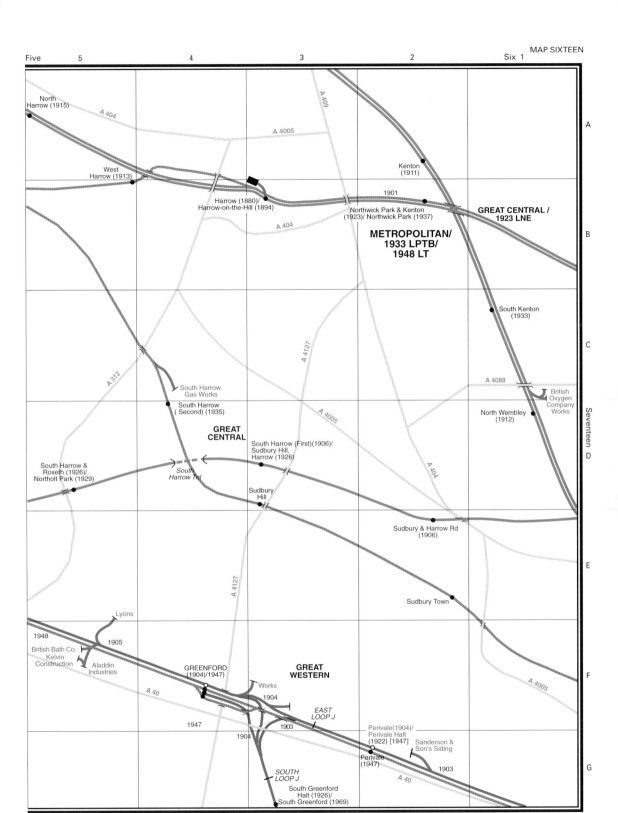

North
Harrow (1915)

A 404

A 4005

A 409

Kenton
(1911)

West
Harrow (1913)

1901

GREAT CENTRAL /
1923 LNE

Harrow (1880)/
Harrow-on-the-Hill (1894)

Northwick Park & Kenton
(1923)/ Northwick Park (1937)

A 404

METROPOLITAN/
1933 LPTB/
1948 LT

South Kenton
(1933)

A 312

A 4127

A 4088

British
Oxygen
Company
Works

South Harrow
Gas Works

South Harrow
(Second) (1935)

A 4005

North Wembley
(1912)

GREAT
CENTRAL

South Harrow (First)(1906)/
Sudbury Hill,
Harrow (1926)

South Harrow &
Roxeth (1926)/
Northolt Park (1929)

South
Harrow Tnl

A 404

Sudbury
Hill

Sudbury & Harrow Rd
(1906)

A 4127

Lyons

Sudbury Town

1948

1905

British Bath Co.
Kelvin
Construction

Aladdin
Industries

GREENFORD
(1904)/1947)

GREAT
WESTERN

A 4005

A 40

Works

1904

EAST
LOOP J

1947

1903

1904

Perivale(1904)/
Perivale Halt
(1922) [1947]

Sanderson &
Son's Siding

Perivale
(1947)

1903

SOUTH
LOOP J

South Greenford
Halt (1926)/
South Greenford (1969)

A 40

Seventeen

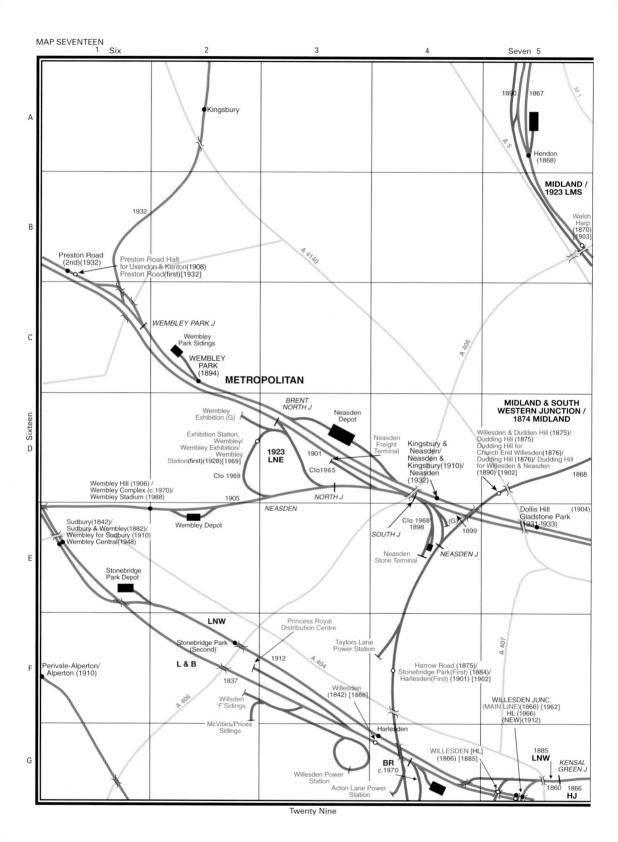

A

1890 1867

M 1

A 5

Kingsbury

Hendon
(1868)

**MIDLAND /
1923 LMS**

1932

B

Welsh
Harp
(1870)
[1903]

A 4140

Preston Road
(2nd)(1932)

Preston Road Halt
for Uxendon & Kenton(1908)
Preston Road(first)[1932]

WEMBLEY PARK J

Wembley
Park Sidings

A 406

C

WEMBLEY
PARK
(1894)

METROPOLITAN

*BRENT
NORTH J*

Wembley
Exhibition (G)

Neasden
Depot

**MIDLAND & SOUTH
WESTERN JUNCTION /
1874 MIDLAND**

Exhibition Station,
Wembley/
Wembley Exhibition/
Wembley
Station(first)(1928)[1969]

Neasden
Freight
Terminal

Kingsbury &
Neasden/
Neasden &
Kingsbury(1910)/
Neasden
(1932)

Willesden & Dudden Hill (1875)/
Dudding Hill (1875)
Dudding Hill for
Church End Willesden(1876)/
Dudding Hill (1876)/ Dudding Hill
for Willesden & Neasden
(1890) [1902]

**1923
LNE**

1901

D

Clo1965

1868

Wembley Hill (1906) /
Wembley Complex (c.1970)/
Wembley Stadium (1988)

Clo 1969

NORTH J

1905

NEASDEN

Dollis Hill   (1904)
Gladstone Park
(1931-1933)

Wembley Depot

Clo 1968
1898

(G)

1899

SOUTH J

Sudbury(1842)/
Sudbury & Wembley(1882)/
Wembley for Sudbury (1910)
Wembley Central(1948)

Neasden
Stone Terminal

NEASDEN J

E

Stonebridge
Park Depot

Perivale-Alperton/
Alperton (1910)

LNW

Princess Royal
Distribution Centre

Taylors Lane
Power Station

A 407

Stonebridge Park
(Second)

L & B

1912

A 404

Harrow Road (1875)/
Stonebridge Park(First) (1884)/
Harlesden(First) (1901) [1902]

F

A 406

1837

Willsden
'F'Sidings

Willesden
(1842) [1866]

**WILLESDEN JUNC
(MAIN LINE)(1866) [1962]
HL (1866)
(NEW)(1912)**

McVities/Prices
Sidings

Harlesden

1885
LNW

**WILLESDEN [HL]
(1866) [1885]**

*KENSAL
GREEN J*

**BR
c.1970**

G

Willesden Power
Station

1860 1866
HJ

Acton Lane Power
Station

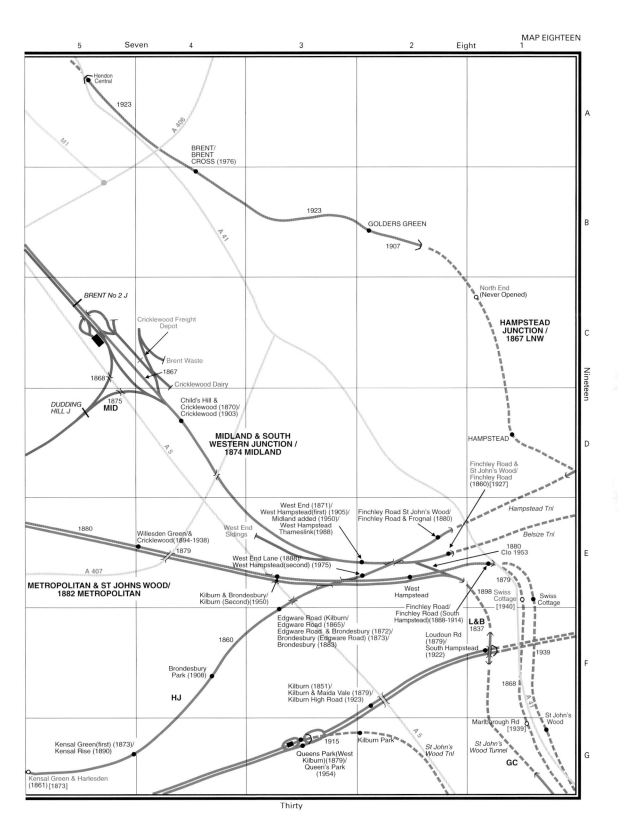

Sixteen

Hendon Central

1923

A 406

M1

A 41

BRENT/
BRENT
CROSS (1976)

1923

GOLDERS GREEN

1907

A

B

North End
(Never Opened)

BRENT No 2 J

Cricklewood Freight
Depot

Brent Waste

1867

Cricklewood Dairy

1868

1875

DUDDING
HILL J

MID

Child's Hill &
Cricklewood (1870)/
Cricklewood (1903)

HAMPSTEAD
JUNCTION /
1867 LNW

C

Nineteen

MIDLAND & SOUTH
WESTERN JUNCTION /
1874 MIDLAND

A 5

HAMPSTEAD

Finchley Road &
St John's Wood/
Finchley Road
(1860) [1927]

D

1880

Willesden Green/&
Cricklewood (1894-1938)

1879

West End
Sidings

West End (1871)/
West Hampstead(first) (1905)/
Midland added (1950)/
West Hampstead
Thameslink(1988)

West End Lane (1888)/
West Hampstead(second) (1975)

Finchley Road St John's Wood/
Finchley Road & Frognal (1880)

Hampstead Tnl

Belsize Tnl

1880
Clo 1953

E

A 407

METROPOLITAN & ST JOHNS WOOD/
1882 METROPOLITAN

Kilburn & Brondesbury/
Kilburn (Second)(1950)

West
Hampstead

1879

1898 Swiss
Cottage

Swiss
Cottage

[1940]

Finchley Road/
Finchley Road (South
Hampstead)(1888-1914)

L&B
1837

Brondesbury
Park (1908)

1860

Edgware Road (Kilburn/
Edgware Road (1865)/
Edgware Road & Brondesbury (1872)/
Brondesbury (Edgware Road) (1873)/
Brondesbury (1883)

Loudoun Rd
(1879)/
South Hampstead
(1922)

1939

1868

A 41

HJ

Kilburn (1851)/
Kilburn & Maida Vale (1879)/
Kilburn High Road (1923)

St John's
Wood

F

Kensal Green(first) (1873)/
Kensal Rise (1890)

1915

Kilburn Park

A 5

Marlborough Rd
[1939]

St John's
Wood Tnl

St John's
Wood Tunnel

Queens Park(West
Kilburn)(1879)/
Queen's Park
(1954)

GC

G

Kensal Green & Harlesden
(1861) [1873]

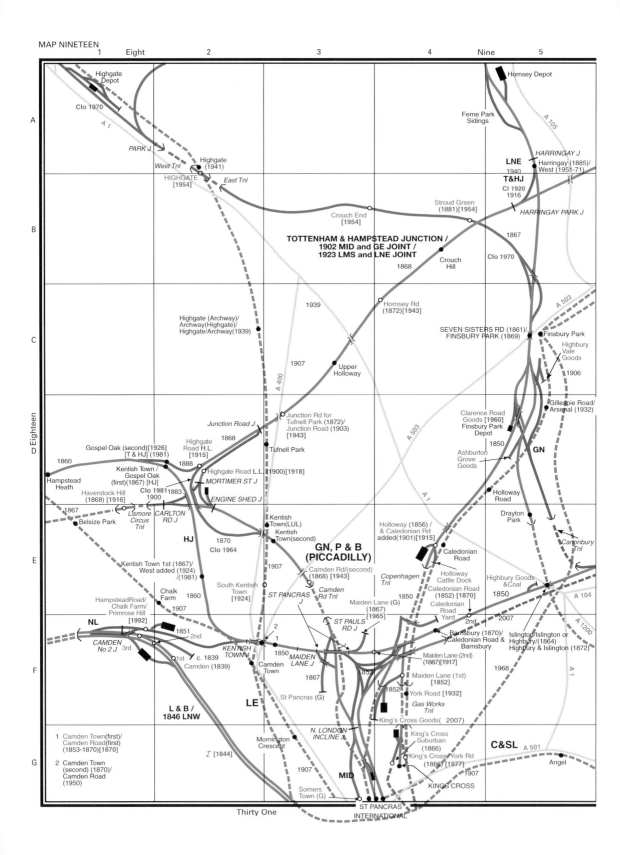

Highgate
Depot

Clo 1970

A 1

PARK J

West Tnl

Highgate
(1941)

HIGHGATE
[1954]

East Tnl

Hornsey Depot

Ferne Park
Sidings

A 105

LNE
1940

HARRINGAY J

Harringay (1885)/
West (1951-71)

T&HJ
Cl 1920
1916

HARRINGAY PARK J

Crouch End
[1954]

Stroud Green
(1881)[1954]

1867

**TOTTENHAM & HAMPSTEAD JUNCTION /
1902 MID and GE JOINT /
1923 LMS and LNE JOINT**

Crouch
Hill

1868

Clo 1970

A 503

1939

Hornsey Rd
(1872)[1943]

Highgate (Archway)/
Archway(Highgate)/
Highgate/Archway(1939)

SEVEN SISTERS RD (1861)/
FINSBURY PARK (1869)

Finsbury Park

Highbury
Vale
Goods

1906

1907

A 400

Upper
Holloway

Gillespie Road/
Arsenal (1932)

Junction Rd for
Tufnell Park (1872)/
Junction Road (1903)
[1943]

Clarence Road
Goods [1960]
Finsbury Park
Depot

A 503

Junction Road J

1868

Highgate
Road H.L.
[1915]

Tufnell Park

1850

Gospel Oak (second)[1926]
[T & HJ] (1981)

GN

1860

Kentish Town /
Gospel Oak
(first)(1867) [HJ]

1888

Highgate Road L.L. (1900)[1918]

Ashburton
Grove
Goods

A 1

Hampstead
Heath

Haverstock Hill
(1868) [1916]

Clo 1981
1900

1883

MORTIMER ST J

Holloway
Road

Drayton
Park

1867

Belsize Park

Lismore
Circus
Tnl

CARLTON
RD J

ENGINE SHED J

Kentish
Town(LUL)
Kentish
Town(second)

Holloway (1856) /
& Caledonian Rd
added(1901)[1915]

Canonbury
Tnl

HJ

1870
Clo 1964

**GN, P & B
(PICCADILLY)**

Caledonian
Road

Highbury Goods
& Coal

A 104

Kentish Town 1st (1867)/
West added (1924)
/(1981)

Chalk
Farm

1860

South Kentish
Town
[1924]

1907

ST PANCRAS

Camden Rd/(second)
(1868) [1943]

Camden
Rd Tnl

Copenhagen
Tnl

Holloway
Cattle Dock

Caledonian
Road
(1852) [1870]

1850

1850

2nd

2007

HampsteadRoad/
Chalk Farm/
Primrose Hill
[1992]

1907

NL

1851
2nd

ST PAULS
RD J

Maiden Lane (G)
(1867)
[1965]

Caledonian
Road Yard

Barnsbury (1870)/
Caledonian Road &
Barnsbury

Islington/Islington or
Highbury/(1864)
Highbury & Islington (1872)

CAMDEN
No 2 J

3rd

1st
c. 1839

Camden (1839)

2

1

1850

KENTISH
TOWN J

Camden
Town

MAIDEN
LANE J

Maiden Lane (2nd)
(1887)[1917]

1968

A 1

A 1200

1867

1852

1852

Maiden Lane (1st)
[1852]

York Road [1932]

LE

St Pancras (G)

Gas Works
Tnl

**L & B /
1846 LNW**

1 Camden Town(first)/
Camden Road(first)
(1853-1870)[1870]

2 Camden Town
(second) (1870)/
Camden Road
(1950)

Mornington
Crescent

I [1844]

N. LONDON
INCLINE J

King's Cross Goods(2007)

King's Cross
Suburban
(1866)

King's Cross York Rd
(1866)[1977]

C&SL
A 501

Angel

1907

MID

1907

KINGS CROSS

Somers
Town (G)

ST PANCRAS
INTERNATIONAL

D Eighteen

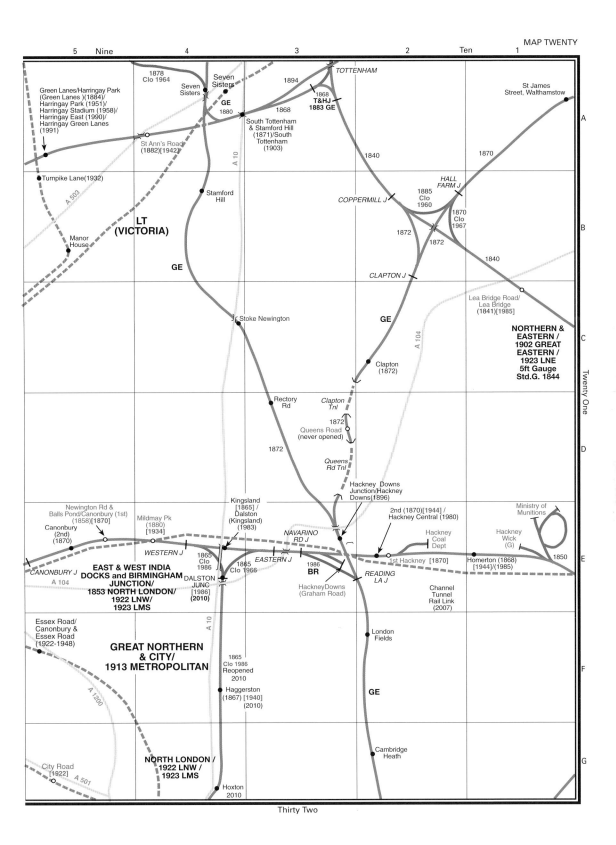

5   Nine   4   3   2   Ten   1

St James
Street, Walthamstow

1878
Clo 1964

Seven Sisters
Seven Sisters

1894

TOTTENHAM

Green Lanes/Harringay Park
(Green Lanes)(1884)/
Harringay Park (1951)/
Harringay Stadium (1958)/
Harringay East (1990)/
Harringay Green Lanes
(1991)

GE
1880

1868
T&HJ
1883 GE

1868

South Tottenham
& Stamford Hill
(1871)/South
Tottenham
(1903)

1840

1870

A

St Ann's Road
(1882)[1942]

A 10

Turnpike Lane(1932)

A 503

Stamford
Hill

COPPERMILL J

HALL
FARM J

1885
Clo
1960

1870
Clo
1967

LT
(VICTORIA)

1872

1872

B

Manor
House

GE

CLAPTON J

1840

Lea Bridge Road/
Lea Bridge
(1841)[1985]

Stoke Newington

GE

A 104

NORTHERN &
EASTERN /
1902 GREAT
EASTERN /
1923 LNE
5ft Gauge
Std.G. 1844

C

Clapton
(1872)

Twenty One

Rectory
Rd

Clapton
Tnl

1872
Queens Road
(never opened)

1872

Queens
Rd Tnl

D

Hackney Downs
Junction/Hackney
Downs(1896)

Newington Rd &
Balls Pond/Canonbury (1st)
(1858)[1870]

Canonbury
(2nd)
(1870)

Mildmay Pk
(1880)
[1934]

Kingsland
[1865] /
Dalston
(Kingsland)
(1983)

NAVARINO
RD J

2nd (1870)[1944] /
Hackney Central (1980)

Hackney
Coal
Dept

Ministry of
Munitions

Hackney
Wick
(G)

WESTERN J

1865
Clo
1986

1865
Clo 1966

EASTERN J

1986
BR

1st Hackney [1870]

Homerton (1868)
[1944]/(1985)

1850

E

CANONBURY J

A 104

EAST & WEST INDIA
DOCKS and BIRMINGHAM
JUNCTION/
1853 NORTH LONDON/
1922 LNW/
1923 LMS

DALSTON
JUNC
[1986]
(2010)

READING
LA J

HackneyDowns
(Graham Road)

Channel
Tunnel
Rail Link
(2007)

Essex Road/
Canonbury &
Essex Road
(1922-1948)

A 10

GREAT NORTHERN
& CITY/
1913 METROPOLITAN

1865
Clo 1986
Reopened
2010

London
Fields

F

A 1200

Haggerston
(1867) [1940]
(2010)

GE

City Road
[1922]

A 501

NORTH LONDON /
1922 LNW /
1923 LMS

Cambridge
Heath

G

Hoxton
2010

1 Ten 2 3 4 Eleven 5

1870

HOE STREET,
WALTHAMSTOW/
WALTHAMSTOW
CENTRAL (1968)

Walthamstow/
Queen's Road
added (1968)

A 112

A 449

A 113

A 12

1856
Clo to
BR 1966

Snaresbrook/
& Wanstead
(1898-1947)

A **TOTTENHAM &
FOREST GATE
(MID and LT & S JOINT)
1912 MID**

Wanstead

1894

A 104

1947

B

Leyton /(Second)
Midland Road
added (1949)

Leytonstone (First)

1856

Clo to
BR
1966

Leytonstone
(Second)/
High Road
added (1949)

A 12

Stratford TMD
(2001 - 2007)

C

1856 To LPTB 1947 1894

Eurostar
Depot

1871

Temple
Mills Yard

Low Leyton /
Leyton(First)
(1867)

A 11

**LONDON PASSENGER TRANSPORT BOARD/
1948 LONDON TRANSPORT
(CENTRAL)**

D Twenty

Clo
1971

Wanstead
Park

1840

LOUGHTON J

Stratford
Freightliner
Terminal

GE
1881

CHOBHAM
FARM J

1839

Forest
Gate (1840)

**EASTERN
COUNTIES**

1840

A 118

HIGH
MEADS J

Stratford
International
2009

1st (1856)[1866]
Victoria Park

GE
1893

1881

Clo 1969
1854

STRATFORD

Maryland Point(1873)/
Maryland (1940)

2007

E

Hackney Wick
(1980)

1854

LEA J

1854

EASTERN J

CHANNELSEA J

EC

1854

Stratford L.L. (1854)

SOUTHERN J

Thornton Fields
Carriage Sidings
(1928 - 2008)

1854

Stratford Bridge (1847)/
1st Stratford Market
(1880)[1892]/Stratford
Market (2010)

**LONDON, TILBURY
& SOUTHEND
(MET DIST)**

Clo 1981

WESTERN J

Pudding
Mill Lane
(1996)

2nd Stratford
Market
(1892)[1957]/
(West Ham)
(1898-1923)

F

A 12

Old Ford
(1867) [1945]

Clo
1993
MID
1892

1839

EC

Stratford
Market
Depot

Stratford
Market (G)
(c. 1880)

Abbey Road
(2010)

1850

Bow
(G)

Plaistow
Loco
Works

Plaistow
[MET DIST]

Victoria Park
& Bow
(1848)[1850]

BOW J

WestHam
(first)(1901)/West
Ham Manor Road
(1924-1969)

A 11

1846

EC & TJ

Old Ford (1865)/
Coborn Rd 1st
(1879)[1883]

Plaistow
[1962]

G

TILBURY J

Bow Rd 2nd
(1892)[1949]

Bow [1944]/
Bow Church(1987)

(HL) (1901)

Coborn Road
(2nd)(1883)/
Coborn Road for
Lr Old Ford
[1946]

Bow & Bromley
[1850]

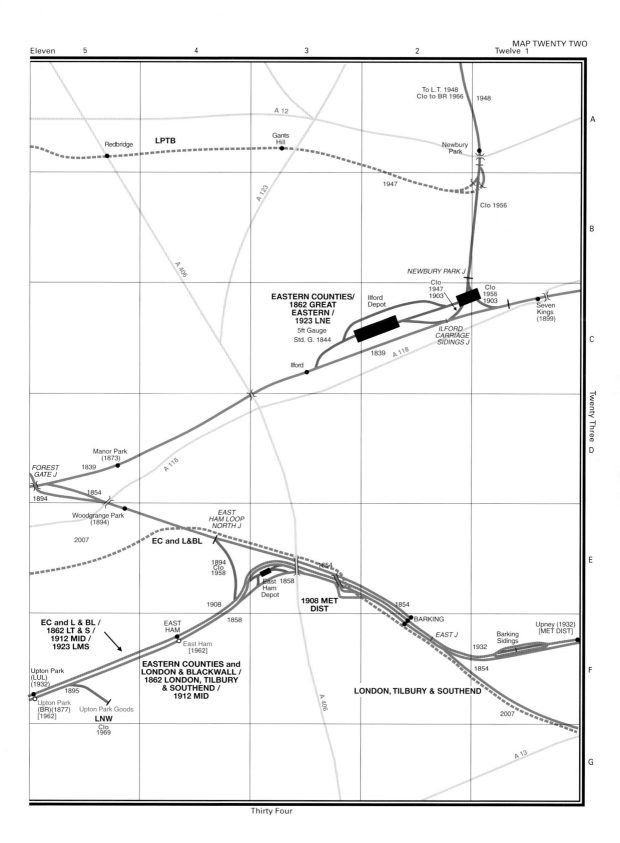

A 12

LPTB

Redbridge

Gants
Hill

A 123

A 406

To L.T. 1948
Clo to BR 1966

1948

Newbury
Park

1947

Clo 1956

NEWBURY PARK J

Clo
1947
1903

Clo
1956
1903

Seven
Kings
(1899)

**EASTERN COUNTIES/
1862 GREAT
EASTERN /
1923 LNE**
5ft Gauge
Std. G. 1844

Ilford
Depot

*ILFORD
CARRIAGE
SIDINGS J*

Ilford

1839 A 118

Manor Park
(1873)

1839

A 118

*FOREST
GATE J*

1854

1894

Woodgrange Park
(1894)

2007

*EAST
HAM LOOP
NORTH J*

EC and L&BL

1894
Clo
1958

1854

East 1858
Ham Depot

**1908 MET
DIST**

1854

BARKING

1908

**EC and L & BL /
1862 LT & S /
1912 MID /
1923 LMS**

EAST
HAM

1858

*East Ham
[1962]*

**EASTERN COUNTIES and
LONDON & BLACKWALL /
1862 LONDON, TILBURY
& SOUTHEND /
1912 MID**

EAST J

1932

Barking
Sidings

Upney (1932)
[MET DIST]

LONDON, TILBURY & SOUTHEND

1854

Upton Park
(LUL)
(1932)

1895

Upton Park
(BR)(1877)
[1962]

Upton Park Goods

LNW
Clo
1969

A 406

2007

A 13

A
B
C
D
E
F
G

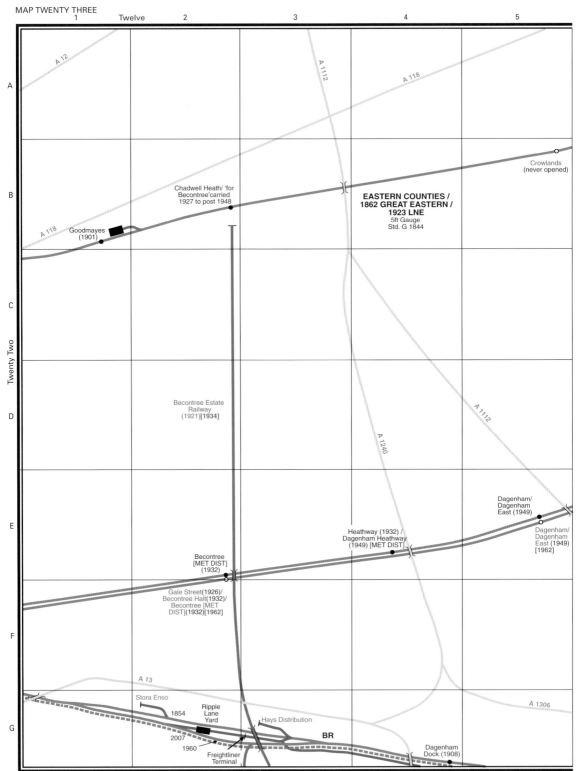

Twenty Two

A 12

A 1112

A 118

Crowlands
(never opened)

Chadwell Heath/ 'for
Becontree'carried
1927 to post 1948

**EASTERN COUNTIES /
1862 GREAT EASTERN /
1923 LNE**
5ft Gauge
Std. G 1844

A 118

Goodmayes
(1901)

Becontree Estate
Railway
(1921)[1934]

A 1112

A 1240

Dagenham/
Dagenham
East (1949)

Dagenham/
Dagenham
East (1949)
[1962]

Heathway (1932) /
Dagenham Heathway
(1949) [MET DIST]

Becontree
[MET DIST]
(1932)

Gale Street(1926)/
Becontree Halt(1932)/
Becontree [MET
DIST](1932)[1962]

A 13

Stora Enso

A 1306

1854

Ripple
Lane
Yard

Hays Distribution

2007

BR

1960

Freightliner
Terminal

Dagenham
Dock (1908)

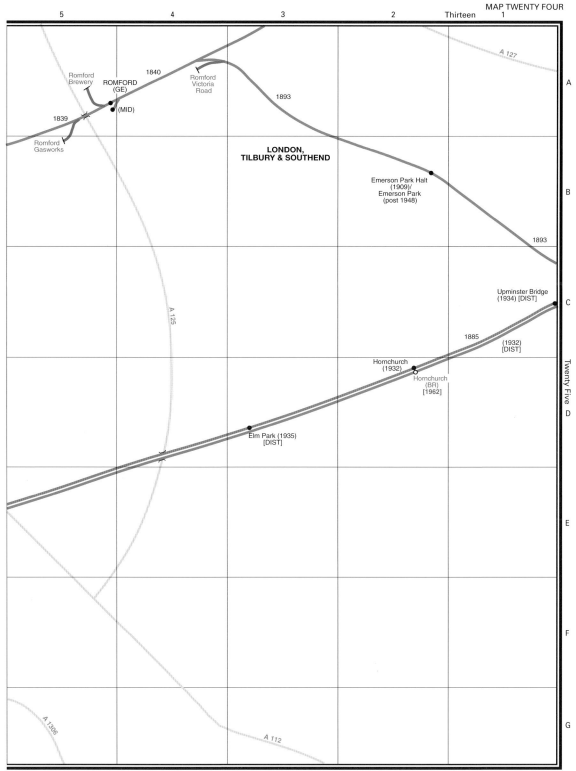

5   4   3   2   Thirteen   1

A 127

A

Romford
Brewery
1840
ROMFORD
(GE)
Romford
Victoria
Road
1893
(MID)
1839

Romford
Gasworks

LONDON,
TILBURY & SOUTHEND

Emerson Park Halt
(1909)/
Emerson Park
(post 1948)

B

1893

Upminster Bridge
(1934) [DIST]

C

A 125

1885
(1932)
[DIST]

Hornchurch
(1932)
Hornchurch
(BR)
[1962]

Twenty Five

D

Elm Park (1935)
[DIST]

E

F

A 1306

G

A 112

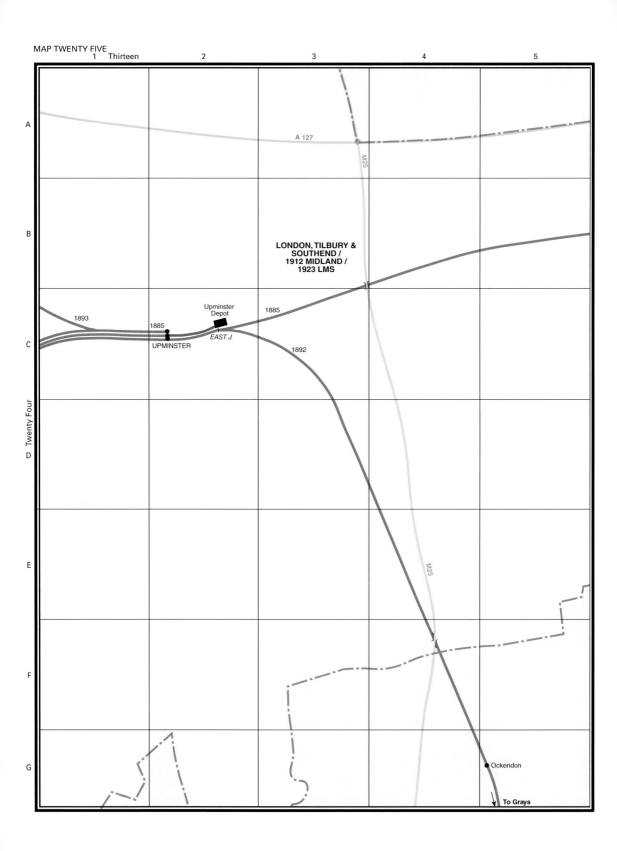

1 Thirteen 2 3 4 5

A

A 127

M25

B

**LONDON, TILBURY &
SOUTHEND /
1912 MIDLAND /
1923 LMS**

1893

1885

Upminster
Depot

1885

C

UPMINSTER

EAST J

1892

Twenty Four

D

E

M25

F

G

● Ockendon

↓ **To Grays**

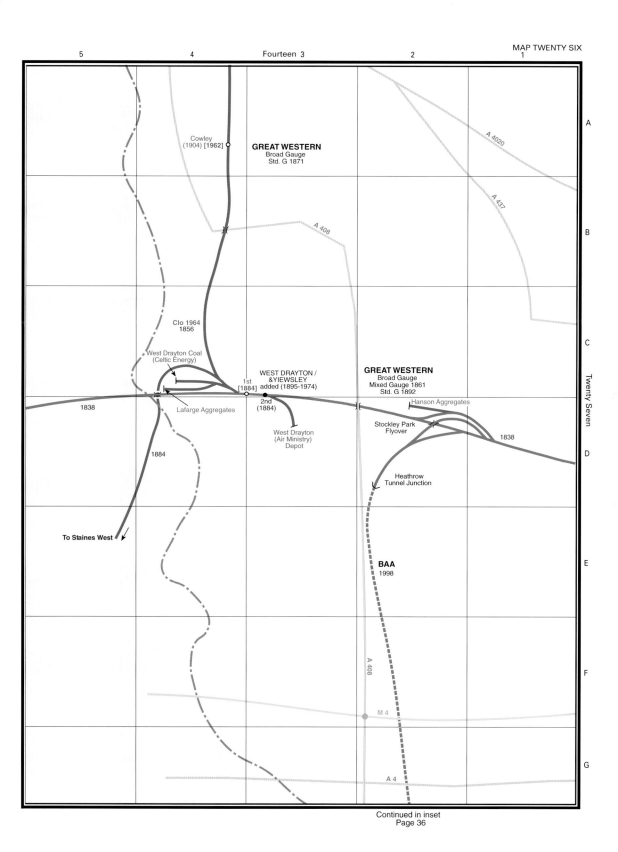

A 4020

A 437

A

B

Cowley
(1904) [1962]

GREAT WESTERN
Broad Gauge
Std. G 1871

A 408

Clo 1964
1856

West Drayton Coal
(Celtic Energy)

C

GREAT WESTERN
Broad Gauge
Mixed Gauge 1861
Std. G 1892

Twenty Seven

1st
[1884]

WEST DRAYTON /
&YIEWSLEY
added (1895-1974)

Hanson Aggregates

1838

Lafarge Aggregates

2nd
(1884)

Stockley Park
Flyover

1838

D

1884

West Drayton
(Air Ministry)
Depot

Heathrow
Tunnel Junction

To Staines West

E

BAA
1998

A 408

F

M 4

G

A 4

Continued in inset
Page 36

1   2   3   Fifteen   4   5

A

A 312

B

A 4020

C

A 4020

Twenty Six

D

GREAT WESTERN
Broad Gauge
Mixed Gauge 1861

Southall
Depot

SOUTHALL
(1839)

AEC Factory

Hayes Gramaphone
Factory

Crown
Oil
Works

British Electric Transformer
Co's Siding

Southall
Gas Works

Std. G. 1892

Margarine
Factory

Quaker
Oats

Tarmac

1838

Hayes (1864)/
& Harlington
added (1897)

Hayes
Sleeper
Creosoting
Plant

Crown Cork
Co's Siding

National
Filling
Factory
(No 7) Hayes

A 437

A 312

E

F

M 4

A 4127

G

A 4

Thirty Six

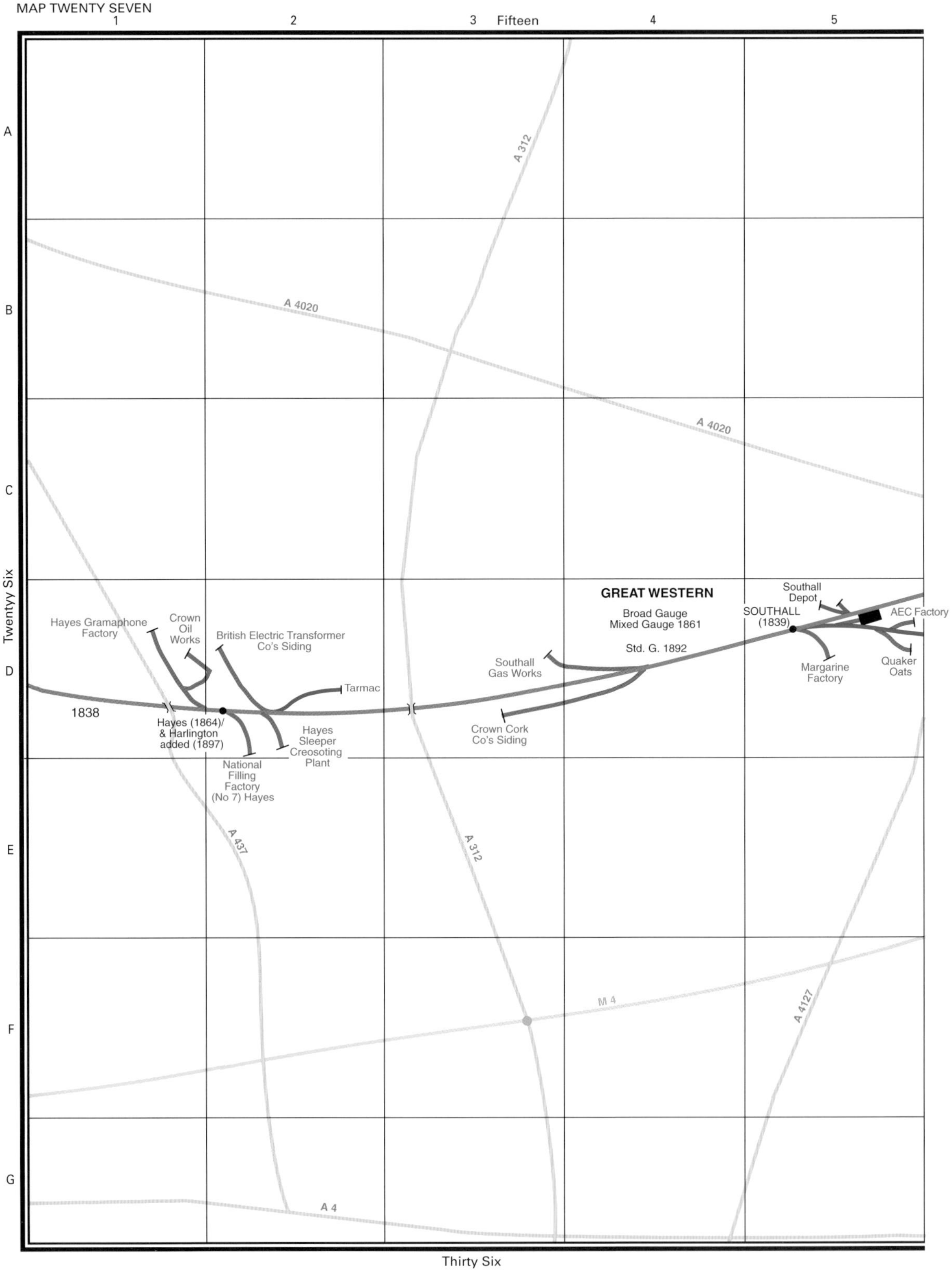

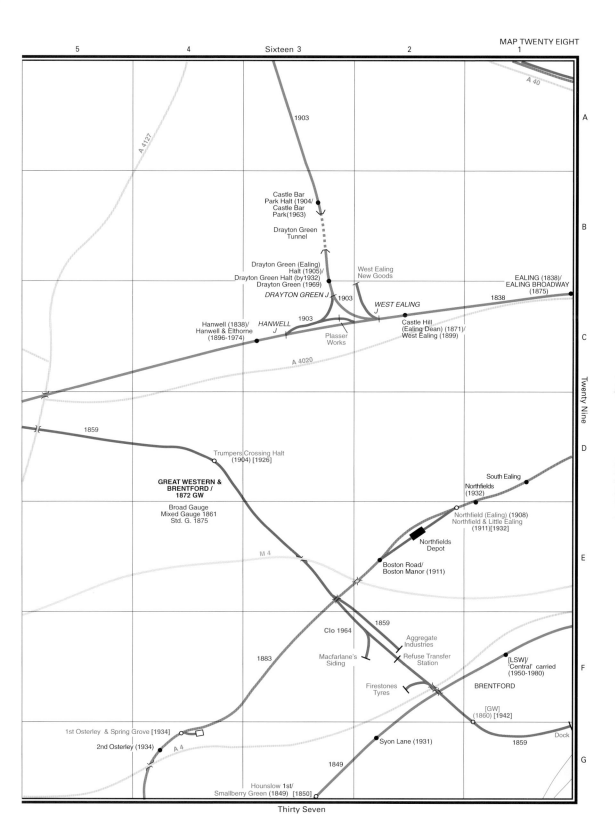

5   4   Sixteen 3   2   1

A 40

A

A 4127

1903

B

Castle Bar
Park Halt (1904/
Castle Bar
Park(1963)

Drayton Green
Tunnel

Drayton Green (Ealing)
Halt (1905)/
Drayton Green Halt (by1932)
Drayton Green (1969)

DRAYTON GREEN J.   1903

West Ealing
New Goods

EALING (1838)/
EALING BROADWAY
(1875)

*WEST EALING
J.*

1838

Hanwell (1838)/
Hanwell & Elthorne
(1896-1974)

1903

*HANWELL
J.*

Plasser
Works

Castle Hill
(Ealing Dean) (1871)/
West Ealing (1899)

C

A 4020

Twenty Nine

1859

Trumpers Crossing Halt
(1904) [1926]

D

South Ealing

Northfields
(1932)

**GREAT WESTERN &
BRENTFORD /
1872 GW**

Broad Gauge
Mixed Gauge 1861
Std. G. 1875

Northfield (Ealing) (1908)
Northfield & Little Ealing
(1911)[1932]

M 4

Northfields
Depot

Boston Road/
Boston Manor (1911)

E

Clo 1964

1859

1883

Macfarlane's
Siding

Aggregate
Industries

Refuse Transfer
Station

[LSW]/
'Central' carried
(1950-1980)

F

Firestones
Tyres

BRENTFORD

[GW]
(1860) [1942]

Dock

1st Osterley & Spring Grove [1934]

2nd Osterley (1934)

A 4

Syon Lane (1931)

1859

1849

G

Hounslow 1st/
Smallberry Green (1849) [1850]

Thirty Seven

1   2   3   Seventeen   4   5

Brentham/
(1911) [1947]
'For North Ealing'
(1920-1938)

HJ
1860
Clo 1892

WEST
LONDON J

1867
LNW

1844

MITRE
BRIDGE J

Park Royal (First)/
Park Royal & Twyford Abbey
(1904) [1931]

Guinness
Brewery

Twyford Abbey
Ammunition Store

ACTON CANAL
WHARF J

1853

1885

Old Oak
Common Goods

Caffin's
Siding

Twyford Abbey
Halt
(1904) [1911]

Park Royal West
(1932) [1947]

Park Royal
(1903) [1937]

OLD
OAK J

EAST
J

A

Hanger Lane
(1947)

1903

National Filling
Factory No 3

NORTH
ACTON J

Old Oak Lane
Halt (1906)[1947]

1868

1853

Old Oak
Common

EAST
J

A

Park Royal/
(Hanger Lane)
(1936- 1947)

A 40

North Acton
(1923) [1947]

LNW

WEST
J

North
Pole

OLD OAK EAST
to NORTH POLE
1863 Clo 1990

British Can Co/
Fiat Eng/ Josephs
Siding

North Acton
Halt
(1904) [1913]

North Acton
(LUL)(1923)

ACTON
WELLS J

GW

MET DIST

Acton
Corporation
Siding

1877

WEST LONDON /
(GW & LNW JOINT)

Broad Gauge
Mixed Gauge
Std. G. 1875

North
Ealing

West Acton

Acton (1868)/
(Main Line)
added (1949)

1917
East
Acton

Mixed Gauge
Std. G. 1875

B

Ealing(1838)
Ealing Broadway
(1875)

1879

East
Acton

Clo 1964

A 40

A 4020

A 4020

1853

A 4000

Acton/
Central
added (1925)

C

Twenty Eight

Ealing Common
/West Acton
(1886-1919)

1879

Ealing
Common
Depot

ACTON TOWN J

Acton
GATEHOUSE J
(1909)

Acton Coal

Rugby Rd Halt
(1909)
[1917]

1833

Mill Hill Park/
Acton Town
(1910)

1857
Clo 1965

Woodstock Rd
Halt (1909)
[1917]

A 402

D

MET DIST

South Acton
(1905)[1959]
Clo
1959

N & SWJ

LSW

Acton
Works

South Acton
(1880)

Acton Green/
Chiswick Park
& Acton Park
(1887)
Chiswick Park
(1910)

Bath Road Halt
(1909)
[1917]

Stamford
Brook (1912)

STUDLAND
RD J

N & SWJ

BOLLO
LANE J Clo
1965
1878

LSW

Turnham
Green

1869

1853

M 4

KEW
EAST
J

1869

1869

ACTON
LANE
J

A 315

Shaftesbury Rd (1873)/
Ravenscourt Park (1888)

Hammersmith (1858)/
& Chiswick added
(1880) [1917]

A 4

E

A 4

Kew1st
[N & SWJ]
[1866]

A 315

Brentford Rd/
Gunnersbury (1880)

A 4

OLD
KEW
J

1862
LSW

NEW KEW J
CHISWICK J

[LSW]/
Kew Bridge
(1868)

LSW
1870
Clo 1932

Kew 2nd
[N & SWT] /
Kew Bridge
(1868) [1940]

F

A 205

Chiswick/&
Grove Park
(1872-1920)

A 316

A 307

G

→ To Richmond

W,S & SW

→ To Barnes

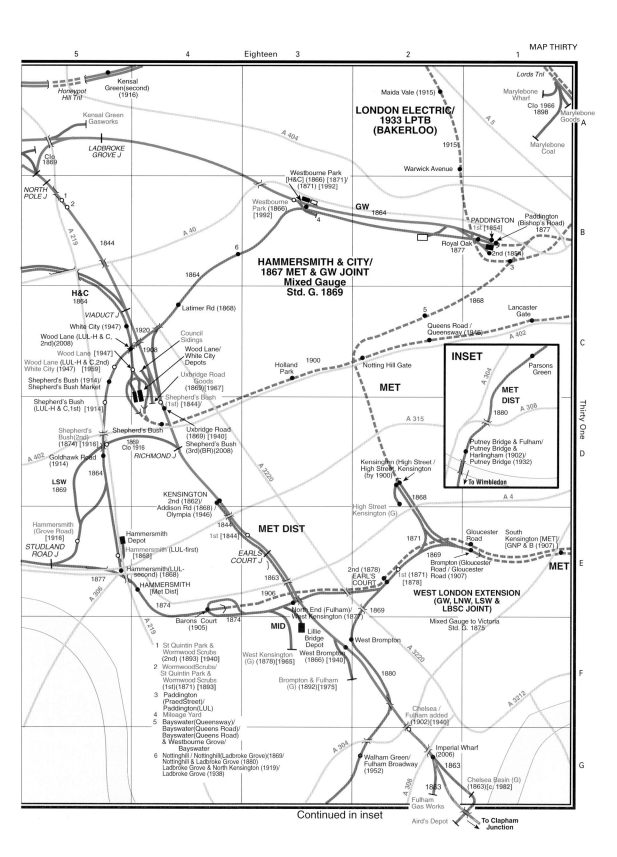

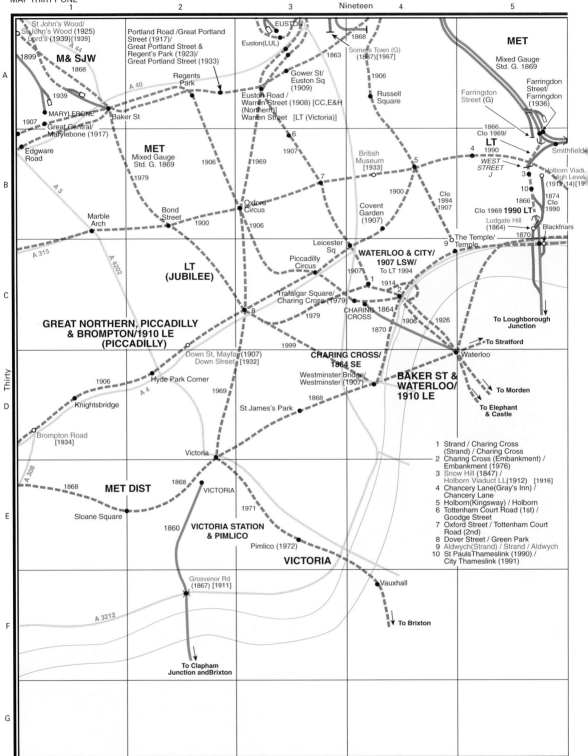

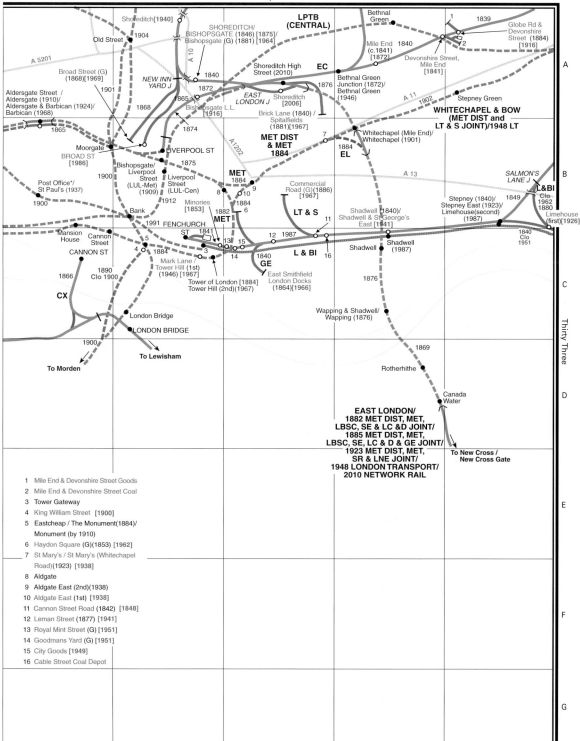

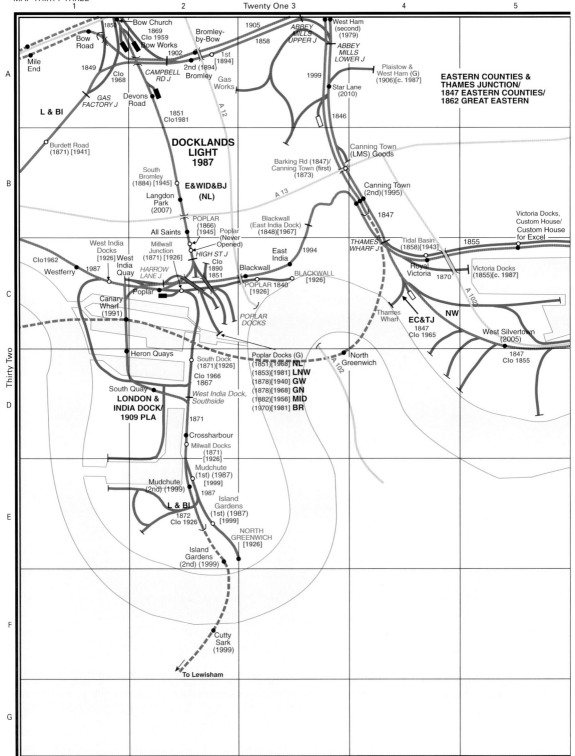

1 2 3 4 5

Thirty Two

A B C D E F G

Bow Church
1869
Clo 1959 Bow Works
1902
Bromley-by-Bow
1850
Bow Road
1849
Mile End
Clo 1968
CAMPBELL RD J
2nd (1894) Bromley
1st [1894]
1905
1858
ABBEY MILLS UPPER J
ABBEY MILLS LOWER J
West Ham (second) (1979)
Plaistow & West Ham (G) (1906)[c. 1987]
1999
Star Lane (2010)

EASTERN COUNTIES & THAMES JUNCTION/ 1847 EASTERN COUNTIES/ 1862 GREAT EASTERN

L & BI
GAS FACTORY J
Devons Road
1851
Clo1981
Gas Works
A 12
1846

Burdett Road (1871) [1941]

DOCKLANDS LIGHT 1987

South Bromley (1884) [1945]
E&WID&BJ (NL)
Langdon Park (2007)
Barking Rd (1847)/ Canning Town (first) (1873)
Canning Town (LMS) Goods
Canning Town (2nd)(1995)
A 13
1847

Victoria Docks, Custom House/ Custom House for Excel

All Saints
Millwall Junction (1871) [1926]
POPLAR (1866) [1945]
Poplar (Never Opened)
Blackwall (East India Dock) (1848)[1967]
THAMES WHARF J
Tidal Basin (1858)[1943]
1855

West India Docks [1926] West India Quay
Westferry
Clo1962
1987
HARROW LANE J
HIGH ST J
Clo 1890 1851
East India
Blackwall
1994
Royal Victoria
1870
Victoria Docks (1855)[c. 1987]

Canary Wharf (1991)
Poplar
BLACKWALL [1926]
POPLAR 1840 [1926]
Thames Wharf
EC&TJ
1847
Clo 1965
NW
West Silvertown (2005)

POPLAR DOCKS
1847
Clo 1855

Heron Quays
South Dock (1871)[1926]
Clo 1966 1867
Poplar Docks (G)
(1851)[1958] **NL**
(1853)[1981] **LNW**
(1878)[1940] **GW**
(1878)[1968] **GN**
(1882)[1956] **MID**
(1970)[1981] **BR**
North Greenwich
A 102

South Quay
LONDON & INDIA DOCK/ 1909 PLA
West India Dock, Southside
1871

Crossharbour
Milwall Docks (1871) [1926]

Mudchute (2nd) (1999)
Mudchute (1st) (1987) [1999]
1987
Island Gardens (1st) (1987) [1999]
L & BI
1872
Clo 1926
NORTH GREENWICH [1926]

Island Gardens (2nd) (1999)

Cutty Sark (1999)

To Lewisham

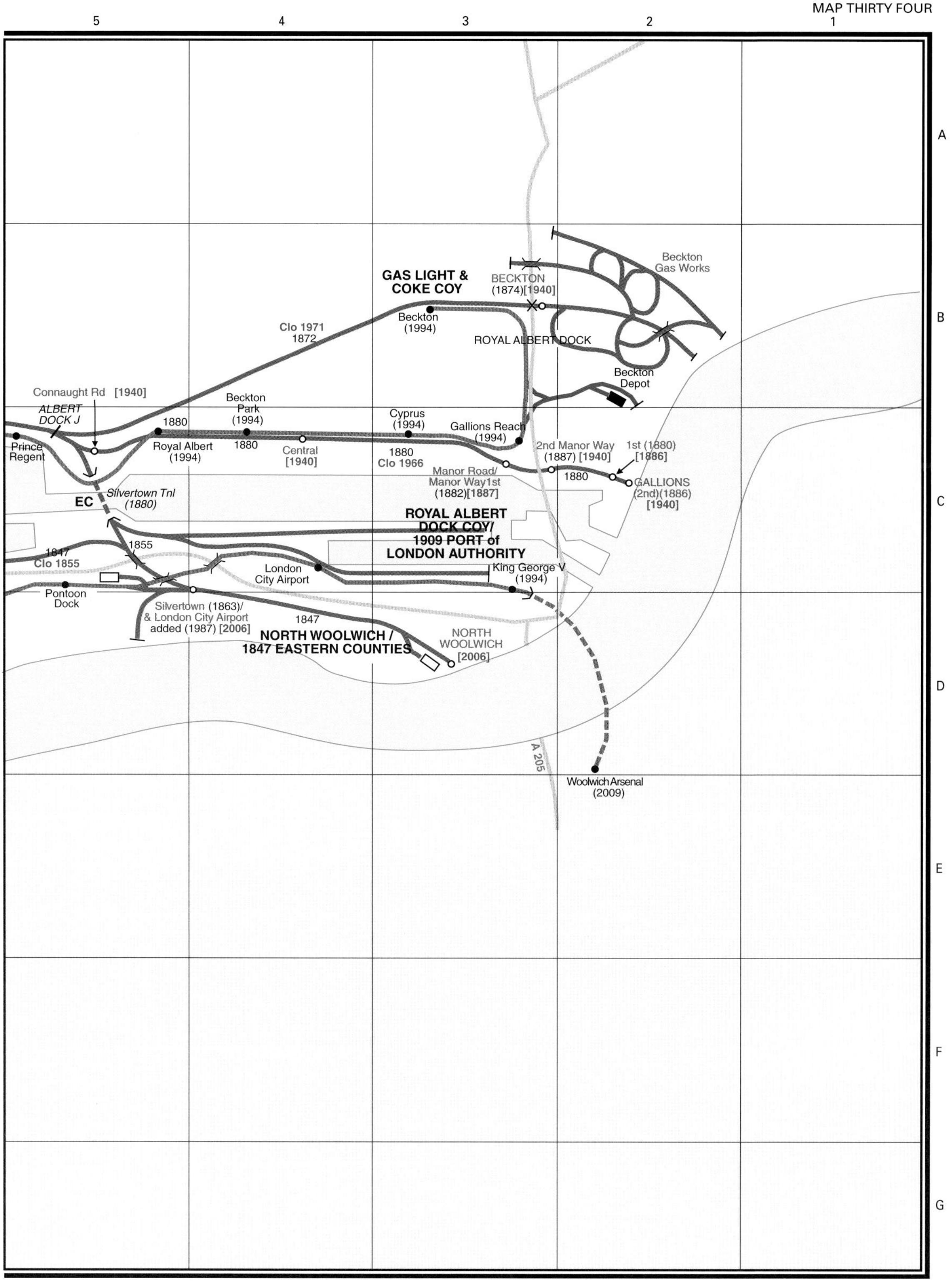

5 4 3 2 1

A

**GAS LIGHT &
COKE COY**

Beckton
Gas Works

BECKTON
(1874)[1940]

Clo 1971
1872

Beckton
(1994)

ROYAL ALBERT DOCK

B

Beckton
Depot

Connaught Rd [1940]
*ALBERT
DOCK J*

Beckton
Park
(1994)

Cyprus
(1994)

Gallions Reach
(1994)

2nd Manor Way
(1887) [1940]

1st (1880)
[1886]

1880
Prince
Regent

Royal Albert
(1994)

1880

Central
[1940]

1880
Clo 1966

1880

GALLIONS
(2nd)(1886)
[1940]

Manor Road/
Manor Way1st
(1882)[1887]

EC

*Silvertown Tnl
(1880)*

**ROYAL ALBERT
DOCK COY/
1909 PORT of
LONDON AUTHORITY**

C

1847
Clo 1855

1855

London
City Airport

King George V
(1994)

Pontoon
Dock

Silvertown (1863)/
& London City Airport
added (1987) [2006]

1847

**NORTH WOOLWICH /
1847 EASTERN COUNTIES**

NORTH
WOOLWICH
[2006]

D

A 205

Woolwich Arsenal
(2009)

E

F

G

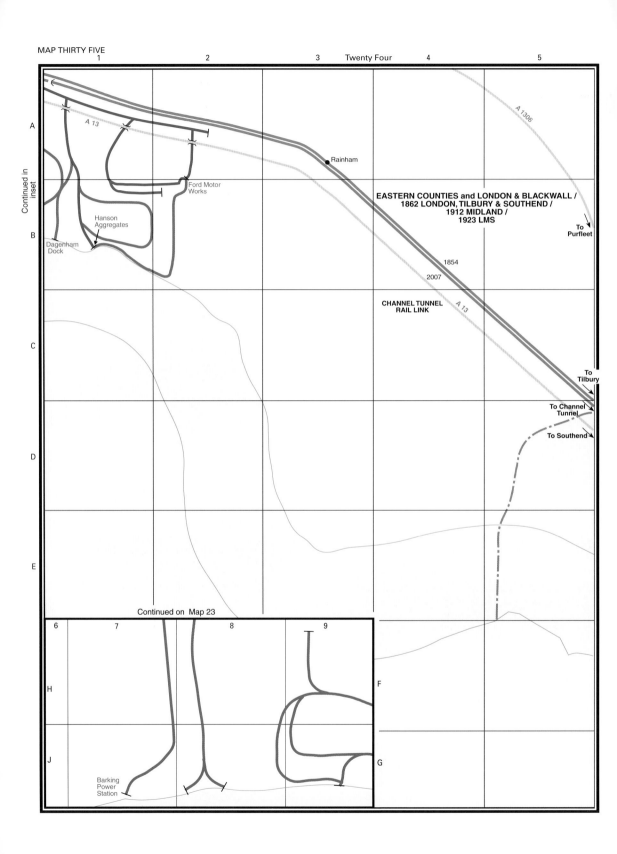

Continued in inset

A

A 13

Rainham

Ford Motor Works

Hanson Aggregates

Dagenham Dock

B

EASTERN COUNTIES and LONDON & BLACKWALL /
1862 LONDON, TILBURY & SOUTHEND /
1912 MIDLAND /
1923 LMS

To Purfleet

1854

2007

CHANNEL TUNNEL RAIL LINK

A 13

A 1306

C

To Tilbury

To Channel Tunnel

To Southend

D

E

Continued on Map 23

6   7   8   9

H

F

J

G

Barking Power Station

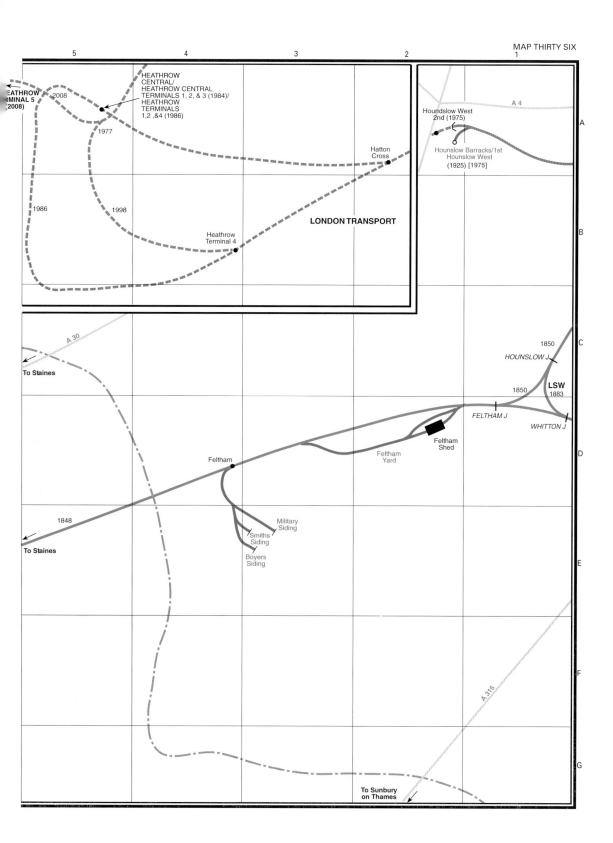

5   4   3   2   1

HEATHROW
CENTRAL/
HEATHROW CENTRAL
TERMINALS 1, 2, & 3 (1984)/
HEATHROW
TERMINALS
1,2 ,&4 (1986)

HEATHROW
TERMINAL 5
(2008)

2008

1977

Houndslow West
2nd (1975)

A 4

Hounslow Barracks/1st
Hounslow West
(1925) [1975]

Hatton
Cross

1986   1998

Heathrow
Terminal 4

LONDON TRANSPORT

A

B

A 30

To Staines

1850

HOUNSLOW J

1850   **LSW**
1883

FELTHAM J

WHITTON J

C

Feltham
Shed

Feltham

Feltham
Yard

D

1848

To Staines

Military
Siding

Smiths
Siding

Boyers
Siding

E

A 315

F

G

To Sunbury
on Thames

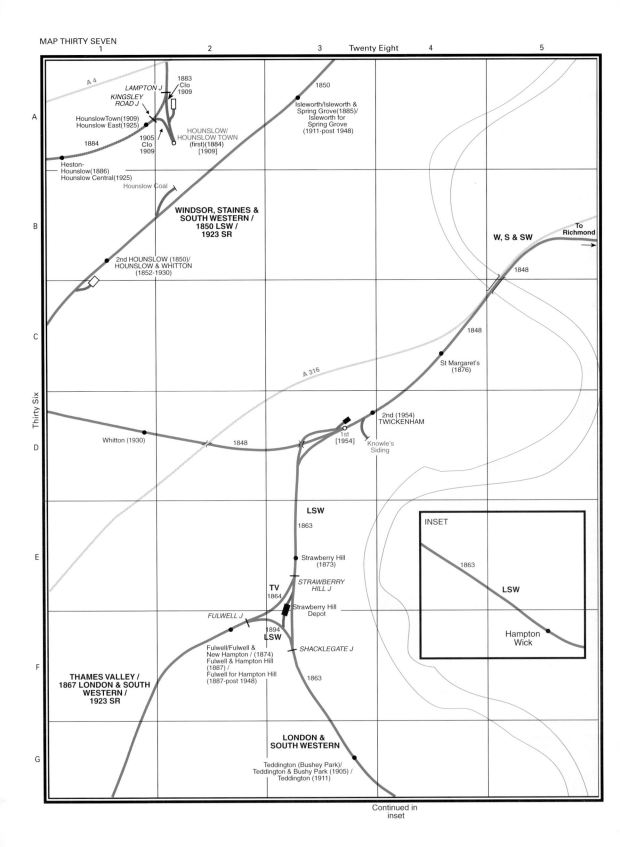

A 4

LAMPTON J

1883
Clo
1909

*KINGSLEY
ROAD J*

HounslowTown(1909)
Hounslow East(1925)

1905
Clo
1909

1884

HOUNSLOW/
HOUNSLOW TOWN
(first)(1884)
[1909]

1850

Isleworth/Isleworth &
Spring Grove(1885)/
Isleworth for
Spring Grove
(1911-post 1948)

Heston-
Hounslow(1886)
Hounslow Central(1925)

Hounslow Coal

**WINDSOR, STAINES &
SOUTH WESTERN /
1850 LSW /
1923 SR**

W, S & SW

To
Richmond

1848

2nd HOUNSLOW (1850)/
HOUNSLOW & WHITTON
(1852-1930)

1848

A 316

St Margaret's
(1876)

Thirty Six

Whitton (1930)

1848

2nd (1954)
TWICKENHAM

1st
[1954]

Knowle's
Siding

LSW

1863

Strawberry Hill
(1873)

INSET

1863

LSW

TV
1864

*STRAWBERRY
HILL J*

Strawberry Hill
Depot

Hampton
Wick

FULWELL J

1894
LSW

SHACKLEGATE J

Fulwell/Fulwell &
New Hampton / (1874)
Fulwell & Hampton Hill
(1887) /
Fulwell for Hampton Hill
(1887-post 1948)

1863

**THAMES VALLEY /
1867 LONDON & SOUTH
WESTERN /
1923 SR**

**LONDON &
SOUTH WESTERN**

Teddington (Bushey Park)/
Teddington & Bushy Park (1905) /
Teddington (1911)

Continued in
inset

Left: Pictured passing West Brompton, Class C 0-6-0 No 31716 heads a southbound SLS special towards Clapham Junction on 15 April 1950. The electrified District Line can be seen on the extreme right.
Ian Allan Library

Below: Class 321 No 321342 calls at Stratford with a service for Witham on 6 June 1989. *Kevin Lane*

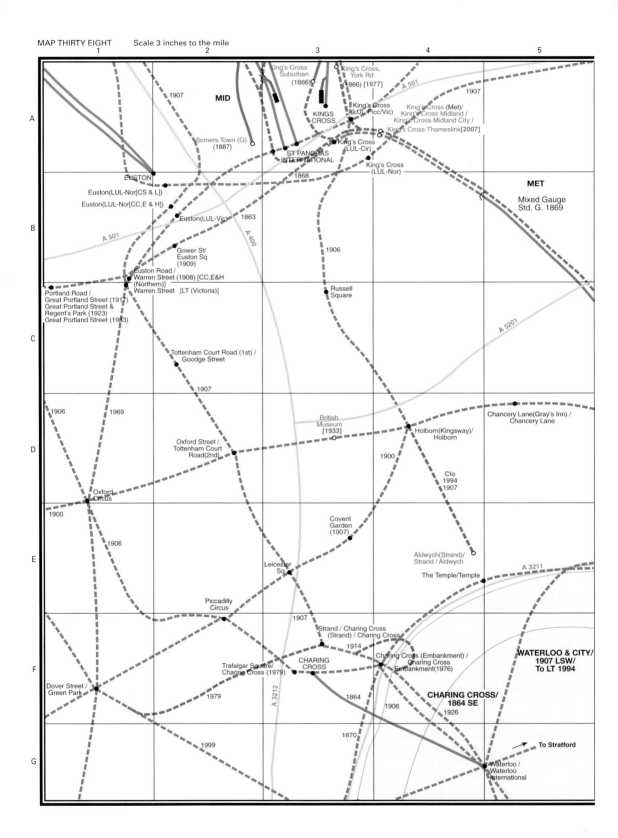

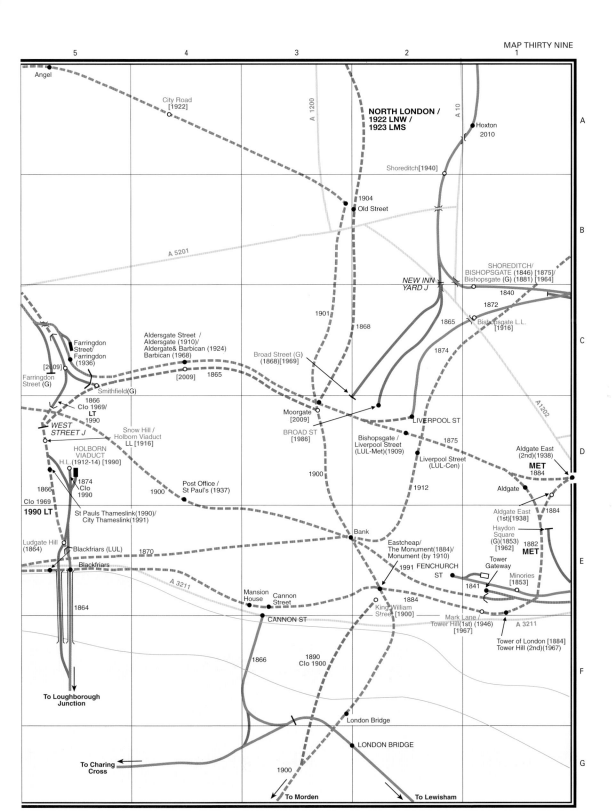

5　　　　　4　　　　　3　　　　　2　　　　　1

Angel

City Road [1922]

NORTH LONDON / 1922 LNW / 1923 LMS

A 1200

A 10

Hoxton 2010

A

Shoreditch [1940]

1904
Old Street

B

A 5201

NEW INN YARD J

SHOREDITCH/ BISHOPSGATE (1846) [1875]/ Bishopsgate (G) (1881) [1964]

1840

1901

1868

1872

Bishopsgate L.L. [1916]

1865

Farringdon Street/ Farringdon (1936)

Aldersgate Street / Aldersgate (1910)/ Aldergate& Barbican (1924) Barbican (1968)

Broad Street (G) (1868) [1969]

1874

C

[2009]

Farringdon Street (G)

Smithfield (G)

[2009]　1865

Moorgate [2009]

LIVERPOOL ST

A 1202

1866 Clo 1969/ LT 1990

WEST STREET J

Snow Hill / Holborn Viaduct LL [1916]

BROAD ST [1986]

Bishopsgate/ Liverpool Street (LUL-Met) (1909)

1875

Aldgate East (2nd) (1938)

HOLBORN VIADUCT H.L. (1912-14) [1990]

Post Office / St Paul's (1937)

Liverpool Street (LUL-Cen)

MET 1884

D

1874 Clo 1990

1900

1900

1912

Aldgate

1884

1866

Clo 1969

1990 LT

St Pauls Thameslink(1990)/ City Thameslink(1991)

Aldgate East (1st) [1938]

Haydon Square (G) (1853) [1962]

1882 **MET**

Ludgate Hill (1864)

Blackfriars (LUL)

1870

Bank

Eastcheap/ The Monument (1884)/ Monument (by 1910)

1841

Tower Gateway

Minories [1853]

Blackfriars

1991 FENCHURCH ST

E

1864

Mansion House

Cannon Street

1884

King William Street [1900]

Mark Lane / Tower Hill (1st) (1946) [1967]

A 3211

Tower of London [1884] Tower Hill (2nd) (1967)

A 3211

CANNON ST

To Loughborough Junction

1866

1890 Clo 1900

London Bridge

F

LONDON BRIDGE

To Charing Cross

1900

To Morden

To Lewisham

G

Stations are listed according to the name applicable at the time of closure or that currently in use. Included are a number of stations where the Network Rail platforms have been closed but those serving the London Underground remain open; these have been treated as effectively two stations. Where possible the opening date of each of the LUL lines at an individual station is also given; in such cases the current line name is included in parentheses.

Station	Map ref	Opened	Closed (passengers)	Closed (freight)
Acton Central	29C3	1 August 1853	Open	1 March 1965 *
Acton Coal	29D4	Unknown	n/a	4 January 1965
Acton Corporation Siding	29A3	unknown	n/a	unknown
Acton Green	see Chiswick Park; renamed Chiswick Park & Acton Green March 1887			
Acton Lane Power Station	29A2	unknown	n/a	March 1981
Acton Main Line	29B3	1 February 1868	Open	n/a
Acton (GWR)	see Acton Main Line; renamed 1 November 1949			
Acton (LNWR)	see Acton Central; renamed 1 November 1925			
Acton Town	29D2	1 July 1879	Open	n/a
Addison Road	see Kensington Olympia; renamed 19 December 1946			
AEC Factory (Southall)	27D3	Unknown	n/a	unknown
Aggregate Industries	28F2	Unknown	n/a	Open
Aird's Depot	30G2	unknown	n/a	unknown
Aladdin Industries	16F5	unknown	n/a	unknown
Aldgate	32B4 / 39D1	18 November 1876	Open	n/a
Aldgate East (first)	32B3 / 39D1	6 October 1884	31 October 1938	n/a
Aldgate East (second)	32B3 / 39D1	31 October 1938	Open	n/a
Aldersgate & Barbican	see Barbican; renamed Barbican 1 December 1968			
Aldersgate Street	see Barbican; renamed Aldersgate 1 November 1910			
Aldersgate	see Barbican; renamed Aldersgate & Barbican 24 October 1924			
Aldwych	31C4 / 38E4	30 November 1907	30 September 1994	n/a
Alexandra Palace (first)	9F1	24 May 1873	5 July 1954	n/a
	Note: Alexandra Palace closed temporarily on more than 10 occasions during its existence			
Alexandra Palace (Muswell Hill)	see Muswell Hill; renamed 1 May 1875			
Alexandra Palace (second)	9F2	1 May 1859	Open	24 January 1966 *
Alexandra Park	see Alexandra Palace; known as Alexandra Park between March 1891 and April 1892			
All Saints	33B2	31 August 1987	Open	n/a
Alperton	17F1	28 June 1903	Open	n/a
Angel	19G5 / 39A5	17 November 1901	Open	n/a
	Note: Station closed 9 August 1922 to 20 April 1924 and 9 August 1992 to 19 October 1992 (southbound only)			
Angel Road	10D4	15 September 1840	Open	unknown
Archway	19C2	22 June 1907	Open	n/a
Archway (Highgate)	see Archway; renamed Highgate (Archway) 19 January 1942			
Arnos Grove	9D1	19 September 1932	Open	n/a
Arsenal	19D5	15 December 1906	Open	n/a
Ashburton Grove Goods	19D5	1876	n/a	1960
Baker Street (LUL — Bakerloo)	31A1	10 March 1906	Open	n/a
Baker Street (LUL — Metropolitan)	31A1	10 January 1863	Open	n/a
Bank (Central)	32B4 / 39E3	30 July 1900	Open	n/a
Bank (CSL)	32B4 / 39E3	25 February 1900	Open	n/a
Bank (DLR)	32B4 / 39E3	29 July 1991	Open	n/a
Bank (W&C)	32B4 / 39E3	8 August 1898	Open	n/a
	Note: Waterloo & City line closed for refurbishment and other reasons on a number of occasions, including 14 December 1940 to 3 March 1941, 11 May 1941 to 26 May 1941, 8 August 1992 to 6 September 1992, 29 May 1993 to 19 July 1993, 31 March 1994 to 5 April 1994 and 1 April 2006 to 11 September 2006; line transferred to LUL 1 April 1994			
Barbican	32B5 / 39B5	23 December 1865	Open	
Barking	22F2	13 April 1854	Open	1 April 1957
Barking Power Station	35G1	1925	n/a	1981
Barking Road	see Canning Town (first); renamed 1 July 1873			
Barkingside	12G4	1 May 1903	Open	4 October 1965
	Note: Station closed from 22 May 1916 to 1 July 1919			
Barnet	see New Barnet; renamed 1 May 1884			
Barnsbury (first)	19F4	10 June 1852	21 November 1870	n/a
Barnsbury (second)	see Caledonian Road & Barnsbury; renamed 22 May 1893			
Baron's Court (LUL — District)	30E4	9 October 1905	Open	n/a
Baron's Court (LUL — Piccadilly)	30E4	15 December 1906	Open	n/a
Bath Road Halt	29D4	8 April 1909	1 January 1917	n/a
Bayswater (Queens Road) & Westbourne Grove	see Bayswater; '(Queens Road) & Westbourne Grove' carried 20 July 1922 to 1933			
Bayswater (Queens Road)	see Bayswater; date renamed unknown			
Bayswater (Queensway)	see Bayswater; date renamed unknown			
Bayswater	30B2	1 October 1868	Open	n/a
Beckton	34B3	17 March 1873	29 December 1940	March 1930 *
	Note: Station closed for brief period after 7 September 1940 prior to final closure			
Beckton (DLR)	34B3	28 March 1994	Open	n/a
Beckton Gas Works	34B2	1872	n/a	1971
Beckton Park	34C4	28 March 1994	Open	n/a
Becontree (BR)	23E2	28 June 1926	15 June 1962	n/a
Becontree (LUL)	23E2	12 September 1932	Open	n/a
Becontree Halt	see Becontree; renamed 12 September 1932			
Belmont	6F4	12 September 1932	5 October 1964	n/a
Belsize Park	19E1	22 June 1907	Open	n/a
Bethnal Green (BR)	32A2	24 May 1872	Open	n/a

Station	Map ref	Opened	Closed (passengers)	Closed (freight)
Bethnal Green Junction	*see Bethnal Green (BR); renamed December 1946*			
Bethnal Green (LUL)	32A2	4 December 1946	Open	n/a
Bishopsgate (first)	32A4 / 39C1	1 July 1840	1 November 1875	n/a
Bishopsgate (Goods)	32A4 / 39C1	1882	n/a	5 December 1964
Bishopsgate (LUL — Metropolitan)	*see Liverpool Street (LUL — Metropolitan); renamed 1 November 1909*			
Bishopsgate (LUL)	*see Liverpool Street (LUL); renamed 1 November 1909*			
Bishopsgate Low Level	32A4 / 39C1	4 November 1872	22 May 1916	n/a
Blackfriars (BR)	31C5	10 May 1886	Open	n/a
	Note: Eastern terminal platforms closed 20 March 2009			
Blackfriars (LUL)	31C5	30 May 1870	Open	n/a
	Note: Station temporarily closed 2 March 2009 in connection with the upgrading of Thameslink and scheduled to reopen in late 2011			
Black Horse Road (first)	10G3	9 July 1894	14 December 1981	7 December 1964
Blackhorse Road (second)	10G3	14 December 1981	Open	n/a
Blackhorse Road (LUL)	10G3	1 September 1968	Open	n/a
Blackwall (BR)	33C3	6 July 1840	4 May 1926	n/a
Blackwall (DLR)	33C3	28 March 1994	Open	n/a
Blackwall (East India Dock) (goods)	33B3	June 1848	n/a	6 March 1967
Bond Street	31B2	24 September 1900	Open	n/a
Boston Road	*see Boston Manor; renamed 11December 1911*			
Boston Manor	28E2	1 May 1883	Open	n/a
Bounds Green	9D1	19 September 1932	Open	n/a
Bow Church	33A1	31 August 1987	Open	n/a
Bow Goods	21G1	Unknown	n/a	Unk
Bow Road (LUL)	33A2	11 June 1902	Open	n/a
Bowes Park	9E2	1 November 1880	Open	n/a
Boyers Siding	36E3	Unknown	n/a	Unk
Brent	*see Brent Cross; renamed 20 July 1976*			
Brent Cross	18B4	19 November 1923	Open	n/a
Brent Waste	18C4	Unknown	Open	n/a
Brentford (GW)	28F1	1 May 1860	4 May 1942	n/a
	Note: Closed between 22 March 1915 and 12 April 1920			
Brentford (LSW)	28F1	22 August 1849	Open	4 January 1965 *
Brentford Central	*see Brentford (LSW); suffix carried 5 June 1950 to 12 May 1980*			
Brentford Dock	28G1	18 July 1859	n/a	31 December 1964
Brentford Road	*see Gunnersbury; renamed 1 November 1871*			
Brentham	29A1	1 May 1911	30 June 1947	n/a
	Note: Station closed between 1 February 1915 and 29 March 1920			
Brentham for North Ealing	*see Brentham; 'for North Ealing' carried 29 March 1920 to July 1938*			
Brick Lane	*see Spitalfields; renamed 1881*			
Brimsdown	3E3	1 October 1884	Open	4 October 1965 *
(Brimsdown) Works	3E3	unknown	n/a	unknown
Brimsdown Power Station	3E3	unknown	n/a	unknown
British Bath Co	16F5	unknown	n/a	unknown
British Can Co Siding	29A3	unknown	n/a	unknown
British Electric Transformer Co's Siding	27D2	unknown	n/a	unknown
British Museum	31B4 / 38D3	30 July 1900	25 September 1933	n/a
British Oxygen Co Works	16C1	unknown	n/a	unknown
Broad Street Goods	32B4 / 39D2	1868	n/a	27 January 1969
Broad Street	32B4 / 39D2	1 November 1865	30 June 1986	n/a
Bromley (first)	33A2	31 March 1858	1 March 1994	n/a
Brompton & Fulham Goods	30F3	1 April 1892	n/a	4 August 1975
Brompton (Gloucester Road) (LUL — District)	*see Gloucester Road (LUL — District); renamed 1907*			
Brompton (Gloucester Road) (LUL — Metropolitan)	*see Gloucester Road (LUL – Circle); renamed 1907*			
Brompton Road	31D1	15 December 1906	30 July 1934	n/a
Brondesbury	18F3	2 January 1860	Open	n/a
Brondesbury (Edgware Road)	*see Brondesbury; renamed 1 May 1883*			
Brondesbury Park	18F4	1 June 1908	Open	n/a
Bruce Grove	9F5	22 July 1872	Open	n/a
Buckhurst Hill	11B4	22 August 1856	n/a	n/a
Burdett Road	33B1	11September 1871	21 April 1941	n/a
Burnt Oak	7E1	27 October 1927	Open	n/a
Burnt Oak (Watling)	*see Burnt Oak; suffix carried 1928 to 1950*			
Bush Hill Park	2G1	1 November 1880	Open	4 May 1964
Cable Street Coal Depot	32C3	1893	n/a	unknown
Caffins Siding	29A5	unknown	n/a	unknown
Caledonian Road & Barnsbury	19 F4	21 November 1870	Open	n/a
Caledonian Road (BR)	*see Barnsbury (first); renamed 1 July 1870*			
Caledonian Road (LUL)	19E4	15 December 1906	Open	n/a
Caledonian Road Yard	19F4	Unknown	n/a	Unk
Cambridge Heath	20G2	27 May 1872	Open	n/a
	Note: Station closed 22 May 1916 to 5 May 1919 and 17 February 1986 to 15 March 1986			
Camden Road (first)	*see Camden Town (first); known as Camden Road 1853 to 1 July 1870*			
Camden Road (second)	19E3	13 July 1868	1 January 1916	n/a
Camden Road (third)	19F2	5 December 1870	Open	n/a
Camden Town (first)	19F3	7 December 1850	5 December 1870	n/a
Camden Town (LUL)	19F2	22 June 1907	Open	n/a
Camden Town (second)	*see Camden Road (third); renamed 25 September 1950*			
Canada Water	32D2	17 November 1999	Open	n/a
Canary Wharf (DLR)	33C1	2 April 1991	Open	n/a
Canary Wharf (LUL)	33C1	17 September 1999	Open	n/a
Canning Town (first)	33B3	14 June 1847	29 May 1994	1 July 1968
Canning Town (second)	33B3	29 October 1995	Open	n/a
Canning Town (DLR)	33B3	5 March 1998	Open	n/a
Canning Town (LUL — Jubilee)	33B3	14 January 1999	Open	n/a
Cannon Street (BR)	32C5 / 39E3	1 September 1866	Open	n/a
Cannon Street (LUL)	32C5 / 39E3	6 October 1884	Open	n/a
Cannon Street Road	32C3	21 August 1842	December 1848	n/a
Canonbury (first)	20E5	1 September 1858	1 December 1870	n/a
Canonbury (second)	20E5	1 December 1870	Open	n/a

Station	Map ref	Opened	Closed (passengers)	Closed (freight)
Canonbury & Essex Road	*see Essex Road; known as Canonbury & Essex Road 20 July 1922 to 11 July 1948*			
Canons Park	6E3	10 December 1932	Open	n/a
Canons Park (Edgware)	*see Canons Park; '(Edgware)' carried 10 December 1932 to 1933*			
Carpenders Park (first)	5B2	1 April 1914	17 November 1952	n/a
	Note: Station closed 1 January 1917 to 5 May 1919			
Carpenders Park (second)	5C2	17 November 1952	Open	n/a
Carterhatch Lane Halt	3E2	12 June 1916	1 July 1919	n/a
Castle Bar Park	28B3	1 May 1904	Open	n/a
Castle Bar Park Halt	*see Castle Bar Park; suffix dropped 5 May 1969*			
Castle Hill (Ealing Dean)	*see West Ealing; renamed 1 July 1899*			
Central	34C4	3 August 1880	8 September 1940	n/a
Chadwell Heath	23B2	11 January 1864	Open	7 December 1970 *
Chadwell Heath for Becontree	*see Chadwell heath; 'for Becontree' carried 1927 to post 1948*			
Chalk Farm	19E2	22 June 1907	Open	n/a
Chalk Farm	*see Primrose Hill; renamed 25 September 1950*			
Chancery Lane (Gray's Inn)	*see Chancery Lane; '(Gray's Inn)' carried 25 June 1934 to date unknown*			
Chancery Lane	31B5 / 38F3	30 July 1900	Open	n/a
Charing Cross (LUL — Northern)	31C4 / 38F3	22 June 1907	Open	n/a
	Note: Station closed 17 June 1973 to 1 May 1979			
Charing Cross (Embankment)	*see Embankment; known as Charing Cross (Embankment) 6 April 1914 to 12 September 1976*			
Charing Cross (BR)	31C4 / 38F3	11 January 1864	Open	n/a
Charing Cross (Strand)	*see Charing Cross (LUL — Northern); known as 'Charing Cross (Strand)' from 6 April 1914 until renamed Strand 9 May 1915*			
Chelsea	*see Chelsea & Fulham; renamed November 1902*			
Chelsea & Fulham	30G2	2 March 1863	21 October 1940	n/a
Chelsea Basin	30G1	1863	n/a	11 September 1981
Child's Hill & Cricklewood	*see Cricklewood; renamed 1 May 1903*			
Chingford (first)	11B1	17 November 1873	2 September 1878	n/a
Chingford (second)	11A1	2 September 1878	Open	4 October 1965
Chiswick	29G3	22 August 1849	Open	18 November 1968
Chiswick & Grove Park	*see Chiswick; '& Grove Park' carried 1 November 1872 to December 1920*			
Chiswick Park	29E3	1 July 1879	Open	n/a
Chiswick Park & Acton Green	*see Chiswick Park; renamed 1 March 1910*			
Churchbury	3F1	1 October 1891	1 July 1919	14 June 1958
	Note: Station closed 1 October 1909 to 1 March 1915; renamed Southbury when reopened 21 November 1960			
City	*see Bank (W&C); renamed 28 October 1940*			
City Goods	32C3 / 39A4	1862	n/a	1949
City Road	20G5 / 39A4	17 November 1901	9 August 1922	n/a
City Thameslink	31B5 / 39D5	29 May 1990	Open	n/a
Clapton	20C2	1 July 1872	Open	7 December 1964
Clarence Road Goods	19D5	1875	n/a	13 June 1960
	Note: Site used for Finsbury Park diesel depot			
Coborn Road (first)	31G1	1 February b1865	2 December 1883	1883
Coborn Road (second)	*see Coborn Road for Old Ford; renamed date unknown*			
Coborn Road for Old Ford	31G1	2 December 1883	8 December 1946	n/a
	Note: Station closed 22 May 1916 to 5 May 1919			
Cockfosters	1F4	31 July 1933	Open	n/a
Colindale	7F2	18 August 1924	Open	n/a
Colney Hatch & Southgate	*see New Southgate; renamed Southgate & Colney Hatch 1 February 1855*			
Commercial Road	32B3	1886	n/a	3 July 1967
Connaught Road	34C5	3 August 1880	8 September 1940	n/a
Covent Garden	31B4 / 38E3	11 April 1907	Open	n/a
Cowley	26A4	1 October 1904	10 September 1962	n/a
Cranley Gardens	8G2	2 August 1902	5 July 1954	18 May 1957
	Note: Station closed 1 December 1930 to July 1932 and 29 October 1951 to 7 January 1952			
Crews Hill	2B4	4 April 1910	Open	1 October 1962
Cricklewood	18D4	2 May 1870	Open	6 October 1969
Cricklewood Freight Depot	18C4	unknown	n/a	unknown
Crossharbour	33D2	31 August 1987	Open	n/a
Crouch End	19B3	22 August 1867	5 July 1954	n/a
	Note: Station closed 29 October 1951 to 7 January 1952			
Crouch Hill	19B4	21 July 1868	Open	n/a
	Note: Station closed 31 January 1870 to 1 October 1870			
Crowlands	23B5	Never	n/a	n/a
Crown Cork Co's Siding	27D3	unknown	n/a	unknown
Crown Oil Works	27D1	unknown	n/a	unknown
Cutty Sark	33F2	3 December 1999	Open	n/a
Cyprus	34C3	28 March 1994	Open	n/a
Dagenham	*see Dagenham East; renamed 1 May 1949*			
Dagenham Dock	23G4	1 July 1908	Open	2 November 1964 *
Dagenham Dock	35B1	1887	n/a	unknown
Dagenham East	23E5	1 May 1885	Open	6 May 1968
Dagenham Heathway	23E4	12 September 1932	Open	n/a
Dalston Kingsland	20E4	16 May 1983	Open	n/a
Dalston Junction	20E4	1 November 1865	To reopen 2010	n/a
	Note: station closed from 30 June 1986 to 2010			
Denham	14B5	2April 1906	Open	n/a
Denham Oil Depot	14B4	1942	n/a	1965
Devons Road	33A2	31 August 1987	Open	n/a
Devonshire Street, Mile End	32A2	20 June 1839	By end January 1841	n/a
Dollis Hill	17E5	1 October 1909	Open	n/a
Dollis Hill & Gladstone Park	*see Dollis; Hill; '& Gladstone Park' carried 1931 to 1933*			
Dover Street	*see Green Park; renamed 18 September 1933*			
Down Street	31C2	15 March 1907	22 May 1932	n/a
Down Street, Mayfair	*see Down Street; renamed unknown*			
Drayton Green Halt	*see Drayton Green; suffix dropped 5 May 1969*			
Drayton Green	28C3	1 March 1905	Open	n/a
Drayton Green (Ealing) Halt	*see Drayton Green; renamed Drayton Green Halt by 1932*			
Drayton Park	19E5	14 February 1904	Open	n/a
	Note: Station closed 5 October 1975 to 16 August 1976			
Dudding Hill	*see Dudding Hill for Willesden & Neasden; known as Dudding Hill November 1875 to 1 February 1876 and 1 May 1876 to 1 June 1880*			
Dudding Hill for Church End Willesden	*see Dudding Hill; 'for Church End Willesden' carried 1 February 1876 to 1 May 1876*			

Station	Map ref	Opened	Closed (passengers)	Closed (freight)
Dudding Hill for Willesden & Neasden	17D5	3 August 1875	1 October 1902	6 July 1964
	Note: Station closed 2 July 1888 to 1 March 1893			
Ealing	*see Ealing Broadway; renamed 1875*			
Ealing Broadway (GWR)	28C1	1 December 1838	Open	n/a
Ealing Broadway (LUL) (first)	29C1	1 July 1879	Open	n/a
Ealing Broadway (LUL) (second)	29C1	2 August 1920	Open	n/a
Ealing Common	29C2	1 July 1879	Open	n/a
Ealing Common & West Acton	*see Ealing Common; '& West Acton' carried 1886 to 1 March 1910*			
Earl's Court (LUL — District) (first)	30E3	30 October 1871	30 December 1875	n/a
	Note: Station destroyed by fire; replaced by temporary station 30 December 1875 to 1 February 1878			
	until opening of Earl's Court (LUL — District) (second)			
Earl's Court (LUL — District) (second)	30E3	1 February 1878	Open	n/a
Earl's Court (LUL Piccadilly)	30E3	15 December 1906	Open	n/a
East Acton	29B4	3 August 1920	Open	n/a
East End, Finchley	*see East Finchley; renamed 1 February 1887*			
East Finchley	8G3	22 August 1867	Open	1 October 1962
East Finchley Dairy	8G3	1928	n/a	1948
East Ham	22F4	31 March 1858	15 June 1962	April 1962
East Ham (LUL)	22F4	2 June 1902	Open	n/a
East India	33C3	28 March 1994	Open	n/a
East Smithfield London Docks	32C4	17 June 1864	n/a	1 September 1966 *
Eastcheap	*see Monument; renamed The Monument 1 November 1884*			
Eastcote	15B3	26 May 1906	Open	10 August 1964
Edgeware Road (Kilburn)	*see Brondesbury; renamed Edgware Road 1 November 1865*			
Edgware (GNR)	5D1	22 August 1867	11 September 1939	1 June 1964
Edgware (LUL)	5D1	18 August 1924	Open	n/a
Edgware Road	*see Brondesbury; renamed Edgware Road & Brondesbury 1 January 1872*			
Edgware Road & Brondesbury	31B1	15 June 1907	Open	n/a
	Note: Station closed 25 June 1990 to 28 January 1992			
Edgware Road (LUL — Metropolitan)	31B1	10 January 1863	Open	n/a
Edgware Road & Brondesbury	*see Brondesbury; renamed Brondesbury (Edgware Road) 1 January 1873*			
Edmonton (High Level)	*see Edmonton Green; renamed Lower Edmonton (High Level) 1 July 1883*			
Edmonton (Low Level)	*see Lower Edmonton (Low Level); renamed 1 July 1883*			
Edmonton Green	10B5	22 July 1872	Open	n/a
Edmonton (first)	*see Angel Road; renamed Water Lane 1 March 1849*			
Edmonton (second)	*see Edmonton Low Level; renamed 22 July 1872*			
Elm Park	24D3	13 May 1935	Open	n/a
Embankment	31C4 / 38F4	10 March 1906	Open	n/a
Emerson Park	24B2	1 October 1909	Open	n/a
Emerson Park Halt	*see Emerson Park; suffix carried 1 October 1909 to post 1948*			
Enfield (first)	2F2	1 April 1871	4 April 1910	1 July 1974
Enfield (second)	*see Enfield Chase; renamed 1 July 1923*			
Enfield Chase	2F2	4 April 1910	Open	1 July 1974
Enfield Lock (first)	3C3	1855	1890	n/a
Enfield Lock (second)	3C3	1890	Open	7 December 1964
Enfield Red Brick Co	3F1	unknown	n/a	1937
Enfield Rolling Mills	3E3	unknown	n/a	unknown
Enfield Town	2F1	1 March 1849	Open	14 September 1959
Enfield (GER)	*see Enfield Town; renamed 1 April 1886*			
Enfield West	*see Oakwood; renamed Enfield West (Oakwood) 3 May 1934*			
Enfield West (Oakwood)	*see Oakwood; renamed 1 September 1946*			
Essex Road	20F5	14 February 1904	Open	n/a
	Note: Station closed 5 October 1975 to 16 August 1976			
Euston (BR)	31A3 / 38B2	20 July 1837	Open	
Euston (CS&L) (LUL — Northern)	31A3 / 38B2	12 May 1907	Open	n/a
	Note: Station closed 9 August 1922 to 20 April 1924			
Euston (CCE&H) ((LUL — Northern)	31A3 / 38B2	22 June 1907	Open	n/a
Euston (LUL — Victoria)	31A3 / 38B2	7 March 1969	Open	n/a
Euston Road	*see Warren Street (LUL — Northern); renamed 7 June 1908*			
Euston Square	31A3 / 38B2	10 January 1863	Open	n/a
Exhibition Station, Wembley	*see Wembley Stadium (first); renamed Wembley Exhibition date unknown*			
Fairlop	12E4	1 May 1903	Open	24 March 1958
Farringdon	31B5 / 39C5	1 March 1866	Open	n/a
	Note: Thameslink platforms closed 20 March 2009			
Farringdon Street (goods)	31B5 / 39C5	1909	n/a	Unk
Feltham	36D4	22 August 1848	Open	9 September 1968 *
Feltham Yard	36D2	1922	n/a	6 January 1969
Fenchurch Street	32C4 / 39E2	2 August 1841	Open	n/a
	Note: Station closed 23 July 1994 to 12 September 1994			
Fiat Engineering	29A3	unknown	n/a	unknown
Finchley	*see Finchley Central; renamed Finchley (Church End) 1 February 1894*			
Finchley & Hendon	*see Finchley Central; renamed Finchley 1 February 1872*			
Finchley (Church End)	*see Finchley Central; renamed 1 April 1940*			
Finchley Central	8E5	22 August 1867	Open	1 October 1962
Finchley Road & Frognal	18E2	2 January 1860	Open	1967
Finchley Road (LUL)	18E1	30 June 1879	Open	1 August 1941
Finchley Road (BR)	18E2	13 July 1868	11 July 1927	n/a
Finchley Road (South Hampstead)	*see Finchley Road (LUL); '(South Hampstead)' carried 1885 to 1914*			
Finchley Road & St John's Wood	*see Finchley Road (BR) renamed 1 September 1868*			
Finchley Road St John's Wood	*see Finchley Road & Frognal; renamed 1 October 1880*			
Finchley West	*see West Finchley; date renamed unknown*			
Finsbury Park (BR)	19C5	1 July 1861	Open	1 April 1968
Finsbury Park (LUL; first)	19C5	14 February 1904	Open	n/a
	Note: Station closed 4 October 1964 to 3 October 1965			
Finsbury Park (LUL) (second)	19C5	15 December 1906	Open	n/a
Firestone Tyres	28F2	1928	n/a	unknown
Forest Gate	21E5	1840	Open	7 December 1970
	Note: Station closed 1 June 1843 to 31 May 1846			
Forty Hill	3C2	1 October 1891	1 July 1919	1 June 1966
	Note: Station closed 1 October 1909 to 1 March 1915; renamed Turkey Street when reopened 21 November 1960			

Station	Map ref	Opened	Closed (passengers)	Closed (freight)
Fulham Broadway	30F3	1 March 1880	Open	n/a
Fulham Gas Works	30G2	c1897	n/a	1954
Fulwell	37F2	1 November 1864	Open	n/a
Fulwell & Hampton Hill	*see Fulwell; renamed Fulwell for Hampton Hill 1 June 1913*			
Fulwell & New Hampton	*see Fulwell; renamed 1874 and again as Fulwell & Hampton Hill 9 November 1887*			
Fulwell for Hampton Hill	*see Fulwell; renamed post 1948*			
Gale Street	*see Becontree; renamed Becontree Halt 18 July 1932*			
Gallions (first)	24C2	3 August 1880	12 December 1886	n/a
Gallions (second)	24C2	12 December 1886	8 September 1940	n/a
Gallions Reach	34C3	28 March 1994	Open	n/a
Gants Hill	22A3	14 December 1947	Open	n/a
George Lane	*see South Woodford; renamed South Woodford (George Lane) 5 July 1937*			
Gidea Park & Squirrels Heath	*see Gidea Park; renamed 20 February 1969*			
Gidea Park	13G1	1 December 1910	Open	7 December 1970
Gillespie Road	*see Arsenal; renamed 31 October 1932*			
Globe Road & Devonshire Street	32A1	1 July 1884	22 May 1916	n/a
Gloucester Road (LUL — Circle)	30E1	1 October 1868	Open	n/a
Gloucester Road (LUL — District)	30E1	12 April 1869	Open	n/a
Gloucester Road (LUL — Piccadilly)	30E1	15 December 1906	Open	n/a
Golders Green	18B2	22 June 1907	Open	n/a
Goldhawk Road	30D5	1 April 1914	Open	n/a
Goodge Street	31B3 / 38C2	30 July 1900	Open	n/a
Goodmans Yard (goods)	32C3	1861	n/a	April 1951
Goodmayes	23B1	8 February 1901	Open	31 July 1962
Gordon Hill	2E3	4 April 1910	Open	n/a
Gospel Oak (first)	19D1	2 January 1860	Open	n/a
Gospel Oak (second)	19D1	4 June 1888	Open	n/a
		Note: Station closed originally 6 September 1926 but used by specials until complete closure on 7 August 1939; reopened 13 December 1980 as a bay platform to serve trains to Barking		
Gothic Works	10D4	unknown	n/a	unknown
Gower Street	*see Euston Square; renamed 1 November 1909*			
Grahame-White Aviation Co	7F1	unknown	n/a	unknown
Grange Hill	12D3	1 May 1903	Open	4 October 1965
Grange Park	2G3	4 April 1910	Open	n/a
Great Central	*see Marylebone (LUL); renamed 15 April 1917*			
Great Portland Street & Regent's Park	*see Great Portland Street; known as Great Portland Street & Regent's Park 1923 to 1933*			
Great Portland Street	31A2 / 38C1	10 January 1863	Open	n/a
Green Lanes (GE)	*see Noel Park & Wood Green; renamed Green Lanes & Noel Park 1 May 1884*			
Green Lanes (T&H)	*see Harringay Green Lanes; renamed Harringay Park (Green Lanes) 30 August 1884*			
Green Lanes & Noel Park	*see Noel Park & Wood Green; renamed 1 January 1902*			
Green Park	31C3 / 38F1	15 December 1906	Open	n/a
Greenford (GW)	16F4	1 October 1904	17 June 1963	n/a
Greenford (LUL)	16F4	30 June 1947	Open	n/a
Grosvenor Road	31F2	1 January 1867	1 October 1911	n/a
		Note: LBSCR platforms closed 1 April 1907		
Guinness Brewery	29A2	1934	n/a	November 1995
Gunnersbury	29E2	1 January 1869	Open	n/a
Hackney (first)	20E2	26 September 1850	1 December 1870	n/a
Hackney (second)	*see Hackney Central; renamed 12 May 1980*			
Hackney Central	20E2	1 December 1870	Open	n/a
		Note: Station closed originally 23 April 1945; renamed Hackney Central on reopening 12 May 1980		
Hackney Coal Depot	20E2	Unknown	n/a	Unk
Hackney Downs	20E3	27 May 1872	Open	n/a
Hackney Downs (Graham Road)	20E3	May 1884	n/a	4 October 1965
Hackney Downs Junction	*see Hackney Downs; renamed 1896*			
Hackney Wick	21E1	12 May 1980	Open	n/a
Hackney Wick (goods)	29F1	25 March 1877	n/a	6 November 1967
Hadley Wood	1D2	1 May 1885	Open	1 March 1950
Haggerston	20F4	2 September 1867	Open	n/a
		Note: Station closed 6 May 1940 to 2010		
Hainault	12E3	1 May 1903	Open	1 October 1908
		Note: Station closed 1 October 1908 to 3 March 1930		
Hale End	*see Highams Park; renamed Highams Park (Hale End) 1 October 1894*			
Hammersmith	*see Hammersmith & Chiswick; renamed 1 July 1880*			
Hammersmith (Grove Road)	30E5	1 January 1869	5 June 1916	n/a
Hammersmith (LUL — District)	30 E4	9 September 1874	Open	n/a
Hammersmith (LUL — H&C) (first)	30E5	13 June 1864	1 December 1868	n/a
Hammersmith (LUL — H&C) (second)	30E5	1 December 1868	Open	1 February 1960
Hammersmith (LUL — Piccadilly)	30E2	15 December 1906	Open	n/a
Hammersmith & Chiswick	29E5	8 April 1858	1 January 1917	3 May 1965
Hampstead	18D1	22 June 1907	Open	n/a
Hampstead Heath	19D1	2 January 1860	Open	n/a
Hampstead Road	*see Primrose Hill; renamed Chalk Farm 1 December 1862*			
Hampton Wick	37F5	1 July 1863	Open	3 May 1965
Hanger Lane	29A1	30 June 1947	Open	n/a
Hanson Aggregates	26D2	Unknown	n/a	Open
Hanson Aggregates	35B1	Unknown	n/a	Open
Hanwell & Elthorne	*see Hanwell; '& Elthorne' carried 1 April 1896 to 6 May 1974*			
Hanwell	28C3	1 December 1838	Open	n/a
Harefield Halt	*see South Harefield Halt; renamed May 1929*			
Harefield Siding	14D4	unknown	n/a	unknown
Harlesden (first)	17F4	3 August 1875	1 October 1902	6 July 1964 *
		Note: Station closed 2 July 1888 to 1 March 1893		
Harlesden (second)	17G4	15 June 1912	Open	n/a
Harold Wood	13F3	1 February 1868	Open	4 October 1965
Harringay	19A5	1 May 1885	Open	1 January 1968
Harringay East	*see Harringay Green Lanes; renamed 8 July 1991*			
Harringay Green Lanes	20A5	1 June 1880	Open	3 February 1964
Harringay Park	*see Harringay Green Lanes; renamed Harringay Stadium 27 October 1958*			
Harringay Park (Green Lanes)	*see Harringay Green Lanes; renamed Harringay Park 18 June 1951*			

Station	Map ref	Opened	Closed (passengers)	Closed (freight)
Harringay Stadium	*see Harringay Green Lanes; renamed Harringay East 14 May 1990*			
Harringay West	*see Harringay; suffix carried 18 June 1951 to 27 May 1971*			
Harrow & Wealdstone	6G5	20 July 1837	Open	3 April 1967
Harrow Road	*see Harlesden (first); renamed Stonebridge Park (first) 1 July 1884*			
Harrow	*see Harrow & Wealdstone; renamed 1 May 1897*			
Harrow	*see Harrow-on-the-Hill; renamed 1 June 1894*			
Harrow Weald	*see Harrow & Wealdstone; renamed Harrow 1837*			
Harrow-on-the-Hill	16B3	2 August 1880	Open	3 April 1967
Hatch End	5E3	c1844	Open	14 November 1966
Hatch End for Pinner	*see Hatch End; renamed 11 June 1956*			
Hatton Cross	36A2	19 July 1975	Open	n/a
Haydon Square	32B3 / 39E1	12 March 1853	n/a	2 July 1962
Haverstock Hill	19E1	13 July 1868	1 January 1916	n/a
Hayes	*see Hayes & Harlington; renamed 22 November 1897*			
Hayes & Harlington	27D2	1 May 1864	Open	2 January 1967 *
Hayes Gramophone Factory	27D1	1909	n/a	December 1968
Hayes Sleeper Creosoting Plant	27D2	6 June 1877	n/a	1965
Hays Distribution	23G3	unknown	n/a	Open
Headstone Lane	5F4	10 February 1913	Open	n/a
Heathrow Central	*see Heathrow Terminals 1, 2 & 3; renamed Heathrow Central Terminals 1, 2 & 3, 3 September 1984*			
Heathrow Central Terminals 1, 2 & 3	*see Heathrow Terminals 1, 2 & 3; renamed 12 April 1986*			
Heathrow Terminals 1, 2 & 3	36A5	16 December 1977	Open	n/a
Heathrow Terminal 4	36B4	12 April 1986	Open	n/a
Heathrow Terminal 5	36A5	27 March 2008	Open	n/a
Heathway	*see Dagenham Heathway; renamed 1 May 1949*			
Hendon	17A5	13 July 1868	Open	1 January 1968
Hendon Central	18A5	19 November 1923	Open	n/a
Hendon Factory Platform	7F3	1918	1919	n/a
Herons Quay	33D1	31 August 1987	Open	n/a
Heston Hounslow	*see Hounslow Central; renamed 1 December 1925*			
High Barnet	1F1	1 April 1872	Open	1 October 1962
High Street, Kensington (goods)	30D2	1878	n/a	25 November 1863
High Street, Kensington (LUL — District ex Met)	30D2	1 October 1868	Open	n/a
High Street, Kensington (LUL — District)	30D2	3 July 1871	open	n/a
Highbury Goods & Coal	19E5	1871	n/a	4 August 1969
Highbury Vale Goods	19C5	1876	n/a	5 April 1971
Highams Park	10D1	17 November 1873	Open	4 October 1965
Highams Park & Hale End	*see Highams Park; renamed 20 February 1969*			
Highams Park (Hale End)	*see Highams Park; renamed Highams Park & Hale End 1 May 1899*			
Highbury & Islington	19E5	26 September 1850	Open	n/a
Highgate (Archway)	*see Archway; renamed December 1947*			
Highgate (GNR)	19A2	22 August 1867	5 July 1954	1 October 1962
Highgate (LUL; first)	*see Archway; renamed Archway (Highgate) 11 June 1939*			
Highgate (LUL; second)	19A2	19 January 1941	Open	n/a
Highgate Road (High Level)	19D2	21 July 1868	1 October 1915	n/a
Highgate Road (Low Level)	19D2	17 December 1900	1 March 1918	n/a
Hillingdon (first)	14E2	10 December 1923	6 December 1992	10 August 1964
Hillingdon (second)	14E2	6 December 1992	Open	n/a
Hillingdon (Swakeleys)	*see Hillingdon (first); '(Swakeleys)' carried April 1934 to date unknown*			
Hoe Street, Walthamstow	*see Walthamstow Central; renamed 6 May 1968*			
Holborn	31B4 / 38D4	15 December 1906	Open	n/a
Holborn (Kingsway)	*see Holborn; '(Kingsway)' carried 22 May 1933 to date unknown*			
Holborn Viaduct	31B5 / 39D5	2 March 1874	29 January 1990	n/a
Holborn Viaduct High Level	*see Holborn Viaduct; 'High Level' carried 1 May 1912 to 1 June 1916*			
Holborn Viaduct Low Level	31B5	1 August 1874	1 June 1916	n/a
Holland Park	30C3	30 July 1900	Open	n/a
Holloway	*see Holloway & Caledonian Road; renamed 6 May 1901*			
Holloway & Caledonian Road	19E4	1 August 1856	1 October 1915	n/a
Holloway Cattle Dock	19E4	Unknown	n/a	1 January 1964
Homerton	20E1	1 October 1868	Open	n/a
	Note: Station closed 23 April 1945 to 13 May 1985			
Hornchurch (LUL)	24D2	12 September 1932	Open	n/a
Hornchurch (LTS)	24D2	1 May 1885	15 June 1962	n/a
Hornsey	9G2	7 August 1950	Open	7 April 1975
Hornsey Road	19C4	1 January 1872	3 May 1943	n/a
Hounslow & Whitton	*see Hounslow (second); '& Whitton' carried October 1852 to 6 July 1930*			
Hounslow (first)	*see Smallberry Green; renamed December 1849*			
Hounslow (second)	37B1	1 February 1850	Open	6 May 1968
Hounslow	*see Hounslow Town (first); renamed 21 July 1884*			
Hounslow Barracks	*see Hounslow West (first); renamed 1 December 1925*			
Hounslow Central	37A1	1 April 1886	Open	n/a
Hounslow Coal	36B2	1932	n/a	1973
Hounslow East	37A1	2 May 1909	Open	n/a
Hounslow Town (first)	37A2	1 May 1883	2 May 1909	n/a
	Note: Station closed 1 April 1886 to 1 March 1903			
Hounslow Town (second)	*see Hounslow East; renamed 1 December 1925*			
Hounslow West (first)	36A2	21 July 1884	14 July 1975	n/a
Hounslow West (second)	36A2	14 July 1975	Open	n/a
Hoxton	20G4 / 39A1	2010	To open	n/a
Hyde Park Corner	31D2	15 December 1906	Open	n/a
Ickenham Halt	*see Ickenham; 'Halt' dropped c1947*			
Ickenham	14D2	25 September 1905	Open	n/a
Ilford	22C3	20 June 1839	Open	6 May 1968 *
Imperial Wharf	30G2	29 September 2009	Open	n/a
Island Gardens (first)	33E2	31 August 1987	3 December 1999	n/a
	Note: Station closed 9 March 1992 to 5 April 1992			
Island Gardens (second)	33E2	3 December 1999	Open	n/a
Isleworth	37A3	1 February 1850	Open	n/a
Isleworth & Spring Grove	*see Isleworth; renamed 1 October 1855 and again as Isleworth for Spring Grove August 1911*			
Isleworth for Spring Grove	*see Isleworth; renamed post 1948*			

London North

Station	Map ref	Opened	Closed (passengers)	Closed (freight)
Islington	see Highbury & Islington; renamed Islington or Highbury 1 June 1864			
Islington or Highbury	see Highbury & Islington; renamed 1 July 1872			
Joseph's Siding	29A3	unknown	n/a	unknown
Junction Road	19D3	1 January 1872	3 May 1943	n/a
Junction Road for Tufnell Park	see Junction Road; renamed 1 July 1903			
Kelvin Construction	16F5	unknown	n/a	unknown
Kensal Green & Harlesden	18G5	1 November 1861	1 July 1873	n/a
Kensal Green (first)	see Kensal Rise; renamed 24 May 1890			
Kensal Green (second)	30A5	1 October 1916	Open	n/a
Kensal Green Gas Works	30A5	1851	n/a	March 1970
Kensal Rise	18G5	1 July 1873	Open	n/a
Kensington (first)	30E3	27 May 1844	1 December 1844	n/a
Kensington (second)	see Kensington Olympia; renamed Addison Road 1868			
Kensington High Street (LUL — District)	see High Street, Kensington (LUL — District); renamed by 1904			
Kensington High Street (LUL — District ex Met)	see High Street, Kensington (LUL — ex Met); renamed by 1904			
Kensington Olympia	30D4	2 June 1862	Open	n/a
Kentish Town (first)	see Kentish Town West; suffix added 2 June 1924			
Kentish Town (LUL)	19E3	22 June 1907	Open	n/a
Kentish Town (second)	19E3	13 July 1868	Open	2 August 1971
Kentish Town West	19E2	1 April 1867	Open	n/a
	Note: Station closed 19 April 1971 to 5 October 1981 as a result of arson damage and 1995 to 1996 for engineering work			
Kentish Town	see Gospel Oak (first); renamed 1 February 1867			
Kenton	16A2	15 June 1912	Open	3 May 1965
Kew (first)	29F1	1 August 1853	1 February 1862	n/a
Kew (second)	see Kew Bridge (N&SWJ); renamed 1 January 1869			
Kew Bridge (LSW)	29F1	1 January 1869	Open	3 April 1967
	Note: Goods known as Kew Bridge South after 26 September 1949			
Kew Bridge (N&SWJ)	29F2	1 February 1862	12 September 1940	unknown
	Note: Goods known as Kew Bridge North after 26 September 1949			
Kilburn & Maida Vale	see Kilburn High Road; renamed 1 August 1923			
Kilburn High Road	18F2	December 1851	Open	5 November 1962
	Note: Station closed 1 January 1917 to 10 July 1922			
Kilburn (first)	see Kilburn High Road; renamed Kilburn & Maida Vale 1 June 1879			
Kilburn (second)	18E3	24 November 1879	Open	n/a
Kilburn & Brondesbury	see Kilburn (second); renamed 25 September 1950			
Kilburn Park	18G2	31 January 1915	Open	n/a
King George V	34C3	2 December 2005	Open	n/a
King William Street	32C4 / 39E2	18 December 1890	25 February 1900	n/a
King's Cross (BR)	19G4 / 38A3	14 October 1852	Open	n/a
King's Cross (LUL – Metropolitan)	see King's Cross St Pancras (LUL – Metropolitan); renamed King's Cross & St Pancras 1925			
King's Cross (LUL – Piccadilly)	see King's Cross St Pancras (LUL – Piccadilly); renamed Kings Cross for St Pancras (2nd; LUL – Piccadilly) 1927			
King's Cross for St Pancras (1st; LUL – Northern)	see King's Cross St Pancras (LUL – Northern); renamed 1933			
Kings Cross for St Pancras (2nd; LUL – Piccadilly)	see King's Cross St Pancras (LUL – Piccadilly); renamed 1933			
King's Cross Midland City	see King's Cross Thameslink; renamed 16 May 1988			
King's Cross St Pancras (LUL – Metropolitan)	38A3	10 January 1863	16 October 1940	n/a
King's Cross (LUL – Circle)	38A3	1906	Open	n/a
King's Cross St Pancras (LUL – Northern)	38A3	12 May 1907	Open	n/a
	Note: Station closed 9 August 1922 to 20 April 1924			
King's Cross St Pancras (LUL – Piccadilly)	38A3	15 December 1906	Open	n/a
King's Cross St Pancras (LUL – Victoria)	38A3	7 March 1969	Open	n/a
King's Cross Suburban	19G4/38A3	1 February 1878	8 November 1976	n/a
King's Cross & St Pancras	see King's Cross St Pancras (LUL – Metropolitan); renamed 1933			
Kings Cross for St Pancras (2nd; LUL – Piccadilly)	see King's Cross St Pancras (LUL – Piccadilly); renamed 1933			
King's Cross Goods	19F4	1852	n/a	1973 *
King's Cross Thameslink	38A3	1 March 1833	9 December 2007	n/a
	Note: Station closed 14 May 1949 to 11 July 1983			
King's Cross York Road	19G4 / 38A3	1 January 1866	5 March 1977	n/a
	Note: Station closed 8 November 1976 to 31 January 1977			
Kingsbury	17A2	10 December 1932	Open	n/a
Kingsbury & Neasden	see Neasden; renamed Neasden & Kingsbury 1 January 1910			
Kingsland	20E4	9 November 1850	1 November 1865	n/a
Knightsbridge	31D1	15 December 1906	Open	n/a
Knowle's Siding	37D3	unknown	n/a	unknown
Ladbroke Grove	30B4	13 June 1864	Open	n/a
Ladbroke Grove & North Kensington	see Ladbroke Grove; renamed 1938			
Lafarge Aggregates	26C4	unknown	n/a	unknown
Lancaster Gate	30C1	30 July 1900	Open	n/a
Langdon Park	33B2	9 December 2007	Open	n/a
Latimer Road	30C4	16 December 1868	Open	n/a
Lea Bridge Road	see Lea Bridge; renamed April 1871			
Lea Bridge	20C1	15 September 1840	8 July 1985	7 December 1970
Leaside Works	10D4	c1917	n/a	c1921
Leicester Square (LUL — Northern)	31C3 / 38E3	22 June 1907	Open	n/a
Leicester Square (LUL —Piccadilly)	31C3 / 38E3	15 December 1906	Open	n/a
Leman Street	32C3	1 June 1877	n/a	7 July 1941
Leyton (first)	21D3	22 August 1856	Open	6 May 1968
	Note: Goods known as Leyton Goodall Road after 1 May 1949			
Leyton (second)	see Leyton Midland Road; renamed 1 May 1949			
Leyton Midland Road	21B2	9 July 1894	Open	6 May 1968
Leytonstone (first)	21B3	22 August 1856	Open	2 September 1955
	Note: Goods known as Leytonstone Church Lane from 1 May 1949			
Leytonstone (second)	see Leytonstone High Road; renamed 1 May 1949			
Leytonstone High Road	21 C3	9 July 1894	Open	6 May 1968
Limehouse (DLR)	32C1	31 August 1987	Open	n/a
Limehouse (first)	32C1	6 July 1840	4 May 1926	n/a

Station	Map ref	Opened	Closed (passengers)	Closed (freight)
Limehouse (second)	32C1	3 August 1840	Open	n/a
Liverpool Street (BR)	32B4 / 39D2	2 February 1874	Open	n/a
Liverpool Street (LUL — Central)	32B4 / 39D2	28 July 1912	Open	n/a
Liverpool Street (LUL — Metropolitan)	32B4 / 39D2	12 July 1875	Open	n/a
London Bridge (BR)	32C4 / 39D2	5 June 1839	Open	n/a
London Bridge (LUL — Jubilee)	32C4 / 39D3	7 October 1999	Open	n/a
London Bridge (LUL — Northern)	32C4 / 39D3	25 February 1900	Open	n/a
London City Airport	34C4	2 December 2005	Open	n/a
London Fields	20F2	27 May 1872	Open	n/a
	Note: Station closed 22 May 1916 to 1 July 1919 and 13 November 1981 to 29 September 1986			
Lords	31A1	13 April 1868	20 November 1939	n/a
Loudoun Road	*see South Hampstead; renamed 10 July 1922*			
Low Leyton	*see Leyton (first); renamed 27 November 1867*			
Lower Edmonton	*see Edmonton Green; renamed 28 September 1992*			
Lower Edmonton (High Level)	*see Edmonton Green; renamed Lower Edmonton post 1948*			
Lower Edmonton (Low Level)	10B5	1 March 1849	11 September 1939	7 December 1964
Ludgate Hill	31B5 / 39E5	21 December 1864	3 March 1929	n/a
Lyons Factory	16E5	unknown	n/a	unknown
Macfarlane's Siding	28F2	1928	n/a	unknown
Maida Vale	30A2	6 June 1915	Open	n/a
Maiden Lane (goods)	19F3	1867	n/a	unknown
Maiden Lane (first)	19F4	7 August 1850	14 October 1852	n/a
	Note: Temporary station occasionally referred to as King's Cross			
Maiden Lane (second)	19F4	1 July 1887	1 January 1917	n/a
Manor House	20B5	19 September 1932	Open	n/a
Manor Park	22D5	6 January 1873	Open	1 January 1968 *
Manor Road	*see Manor Way (first); renamed 1882*			
Manor Way (first)	34C3	July 1881	1887	n/a
Manor Way (second)	34C3	1887	8 September 1940	n/a
Mansion House	32B5 / 39E3	3 July 1871	Open	n/a
Marble Arch	31B1	30 July 1900	Open	n/a
Mark Lane	*see Tower Hill (first); renamed 1 September 1946*			
Marlborough Road	18G1	13 April 1868	20 November 1939	n/a
Marsh Lane	*see Northumberland Park; renamed Park 1 June 1852*			
Maryland	21E3	6 January 1873	Open	n/a
Maryland Point	*see Maryland; renamed 28 October 1940*			
Marylebone (BR)	31A1	15 March 1899	Open	n/a
Marylebone (LUL)	31A1	27 March 1907	Open	n/a
Marylebone Coal	30A1	unknown	n/a	unknown
Marylebone Goods	30A1	unknown	n/a	28 March 1966
Marylebone Wharf	30A1	unknown	n/a	unknown
McVities Siding	17G3	unknown	n/a	unknown
Metropolitan Water Board's Siding	9F2	unknown	n/a	unknown
Mildmay Park	20E4	1 January 1880	1 October 1934	n/a
Mile End (BR)	32A2	27 August 1839	24 May 1872	6 November 1867 *
Mile End & Devonshire Street Goods	32A1	Unknown	n/a	Unk
Mile End & Devonshire Street Coal	32A2	Unknown	n/a	Unk
Mile End (LUL)	33A1	2 June 1902	Open	n/a
Mileage Yard	30B3	Unknown	n/a	Unk
Military Siding	36E3	unknown	n/a	unknown
Mill Hill (GNR)	*see Mill Hill East; renamed 18 May 1941*			
Mill Hill (MR)	*see Mill Hill Broadway; renamed 25 September 1950*			
Mill Hill (The Hale)	7D2	11 June 1906	11 September 1939	29 February 1964
Mill Hill Broadway	7D2	13 July 1868	Open	3 August 1964
Mill Hill East	7E5	22 August 1867	Open†	1 October 1962
	Note: Station closed 11 September 1939 to 18 May 1941			
Mill Hill Park	*see Acton Town; renamed 1 March 1910*			
Millwall Docks	33D2	18 December 1871	4 May 1926	1 June 1925
Millwall Junction	33C2	18 December 1871	4 May 1926	n/a
Ministry of Munitions	20E1	1917	n/a	1920
(National Projectile Factory)				
Minories	32C4 / 39E1	6 July 1840	24 October 1853	n/a
	Note: Station closed 15 February 1849 to 9 September 1849			
Monument	32C4 / 39E2	6 October 1884	Open	n/a
Moor Park	4B3	9 May 1910	Open	n/a
Moor Park & Sandy Lodge	*see Moor Park; renamed 25 September 1950*			
Moorgate (BR)	32B5			
	Note: Station closed 5 October 1975 on transfer to BR and reopened 16 August 1976 after reconstruction			
Moorgate (LUL)	32B5			
Mornington Crescent	19G3	22 June 1907	Open	n/a
	Note: Station closed 24 October 1992 to 27 April 1998			
Mudchute (first)	33E2	31 August 1987	3 December 1999	n/a
	Note: Station closed 9 March 1992 to 5 April 1992			
Mudchute (second)	33E2	3 December 1999	Open	n/a
Muswell Hill	8G1	24 May 1873	5 July 1954 14 June 1956	n/a
	Note: Station closed 1 August 1873 to 1 May 1875, 1 December 1930 to July 1932 and 29 October 1951 to 7 January 1952			
National Filling Factory (No 3)	29A3	unknown	n/a	unknown
National Filling Factory (No 7)	27D2	unknown	n/a	unknown
Neasden	17D4	2 August 1880	Open	April 1958
Neasden & Kingsbury	*see Neasden; renamed 1 January 1932*			
Neasden Freight Terminal	17D3	Unknown	n/a	Open
Neasden Stone Terminal	17E4	Unknown	n/a	Open
New Barnet	1F3	7 August 1950	Open	22 August 1966
New Southgate	8D1	7 August 1850	Open	7 December 1970
New Southgate & Colney Hatch	*see New Southgate; renamed New Southgate for Colney Hatch 1 March 1883*			
New Southgate & Friern Barnet	*see New Southgate; renamed 18 March 1971*			
New Southgate for Colney Hatch	*see New Southgate; renamed New Southgate & Friern Barnet 1 May 1923*			
New Southgate Gas Works	8D1	1858	n/a	July 1962
Newbury Park	22A1	1 May 1903	Open	4 October 1965
Newington Road & Balls Pond	*see Canonbury (first); renamed 1 July 1870*			

London North

Station	Map ref	Opened	Closed (passengers)	Closed (freight)
Noel Park & Wood Green	9F2	1 January 1878	7 January 1963	7 December 1964
North Acton (GW)	29A3	5 November 1923	30 June 1947	n/a
North Acton (LUL)	29A3	5 November 1923	Open	n/a
North Acton Halt	29A3	1 May 1904	1 February 1913	n/a
North Ealing	29B2	23 June 1903	Open	n/a
North End	18C1	Never	n/a	n/a
North End (Fulham)	*see West Kensington; renamed 1 March 1877*			
North Harrow	16A5	22 March 1915	Open	n/a
North Greenwich (BR)	33E2	29 July 1872	4 May 1926	n/a
North Greenwich (LUL)	33D3	14 January 1999	Open	n/a
North Middlesex Gas Works	7D2	1886	n/a	1956
North Wembley	16D1	15 June 1912	Open	5 July 1965
North Woolwich	34D3	14 June 1847	9 December 2006	7 December 1970
Northfield (Ealing)	*see Northfields & Little Ealing; renamed 11 December 1911*			
Northfields & Little Ealing	28E2	16 April 1908	11 December 1932	1932
Northfields	28E1	18 December 1932	Open	n/a
Northolt Halt	15E5	1 May 1907	21 November 1948	n/a
Northolt Junction	*see South Ruislip; renamed South Ruislip & Northolt Junction 12 September 1932*			
Northolt Park	16D5	19 July 1926	Open	10 August 1964
Northumberland Park	10E4	1 April 1842	Open	n/a
Northwick Park & Kenton	*see Northwick Park; renamed 15 March 1937*			
Northwick Park	16B2	28 June 1923	Open	n/a
Northwood	4E2	1 September 1887	Open	14 November 1966
Northwood Hills	4F1	13 November 1933	Open	n/a
Notting Hill	*see Ladbroke Grove; renamed Notting Hill (Ladbroke Grove) 1869*			
Notting Hill (Ladbroke Grove)	*see Ladbroke Grove; renamed Notting Hill & Ladbroke Grove 1880*			
Notting Hill & Ladbroke Grove	*see Ladbroke Grove; renamed Ladbroke Grove & North Kensington 1 June 1919*			
Notting Hill Gate (LUL — Central)	30C3	30 July 1900	Open	n/a
Notting Hill Gate (LUL — Metropolitan)	30C3	1 October 1900	Open	n/a
Oakleigh Park	8A3	1 December 1873	Open	n/a
Oakwood	2G5	13 March 1933	Open	n/a
Ockendon	25G5	1 July 1892	Open	6 May 1968
Old Ford	31F1	6 November 1867	23 April 1945	n/a
Old Ford	*see Coborn Road (first); renamed 1 March 1879*			
Old Oak Common Goods	29A5	unknown	n/a	unknown
Old Oak Lane Halt	29B4	1 October 1906	30 June 1947	n/a
	Note: Station closed 1 February 1915 to 29 March 1920			
Old Street (BR)	32A4 / 39B2	14 February 1904	Open	n/a
Old Street (LUL — Northern)	32A4 / 39B2	17 November 1901	Open	n/a
Ordnance Factory	*see Enfield Lock (first); renamed 1 April 1886*			
Osterley & Spring Grove (First)	28G4	1 May 1883	25 March 1934	n/a
Osterley (Second)	28G4	25 March 1934	Open	n/a
Oxford Circus (LUL — Bakerloo)	31B3 / 38D1	10 March 1906	Open	n/a
Oxford Circus (LUL — Central)	31B3 / 38D1	30 July 1900	Open	n/a
Oxford Circus (LUL — Victoria)	31B3 / 38D1	unknown	Open	n/a
Oxford Street	*see Tottenham Court Road (second - Nor); renamed 9 March 1908*			
Paddington (first)	30B1	4 June 1838	29 May 1854	n/a
Paddington (Praed Street)	*see Paddington (LUL); renamed 11 July 1948*			
Paddington (second)	30B1	29 May 1854	Open	n/a
Paddington (LUL)	30B1	1 October 1868	Open	n/a
Paddington (Bishop's Road)	30B1	10 January 1863	Open	n/a
	Note: Station merged with Paddington 10 September 1933 and '(Bishop's Road)' dropped			
Palace Gates, Wood Green	9E2	7 October 1878	7 January 1963	5 October 1964
Palmers Green	9C2	1 April 1971	Open	1 October 1962
Palmers Green & Southgate	*see Palmers Green; '& Southgate' carried 1 October 1876 to 3 May 1971*			
Park Royal	29A2	25 May 1903	26 September 1937	n/a
	Note: Station closed between 5 July 1903 and 1 May 1904 and between 1 February 1915 and 29 March 1920			
Park Royal (LUL) (first)	*see Park Royal & Twyford Abbey; renamed 1 May 1904*			
Park Royal (LUL) (second)	29A2	6 July 1931	Open	n/a
Park Royal (Hanger Lane)	*see Park Royal (LUL) (second); '(Hanger Lane)' carried 1 March 1936 to 1947*			
Park Royal & Twyford Abbey	29A1	23 June 1904	6 July 1931	n/a
Park Royal West	29A2	20 June 1932	15 June 1947	n/a
Park	*see Northumberland Park; renamed 1 July 1923*			
Parson's Green	30G3	1 March 1880	Open	n/a
Peerless Wire Fence Co	14B3	1933	n/a	1953
	Note: Siding originally opened to serve South Harefield in June 1929 and closed 1 October 1931			
Perivale	*see Perivale Halt; renamed 10 July 1922*			
Perivale (LUL)	16G2	30 June 1947	Open	n/a
Perivale Alperton	*see Alperton; renamed 7 October 1910*			
Perivale Halt	16G2	1 May 1904	15 June 1947	n/a
	Note: Station closed 1 February 1915 to 29 March 1920			
Piccadilly	31C3 / 38F2			
Piccadilly Circus (LUL – Bakerloo)	31C3 / 38F2	10 March 1906	Open	n/a
Piccadilly Circus (LUL – Piccadilly)	31C3 / 38F2	15 December 1906	Open	n/a
Pimlico	31E3	14 September 1972	Open	n/a
Pinner (LNWR)	*see Hatch End; renamed Pinner & Hatch End 1 January 1897*			
Pinner & Hatch End	*see Hatch End; renamed Hatch End for Pinner 1 February 1920*			
Pinner (LUL)	5G2	25 May 1885	Open	3 April 1967
Plaistow (BR)	21G4	31 March 1858	15 June 1962	1 May 1953 *
Plaistow (LUL)	21G4	12 September 1932	Open	n/a
Plaistow & West Ham Goods	21F3	1906	n/a	c1987
Plasser Works	28C3	14 March 1960	n/a	Open
Ponders End	3G3	15 September 1840	Open	2 November 1964 *
Ponders End Gas Works	3G3	unknown	n/a	unknown
Ponders End Shell Co	3F1	unknown	n/a	unknown
Pontoon Dock	34C5	2 December 2005	Open	n/a
Poplar	33C2	Never	n/a	n/a
Poplar (BR)	33C3	1840	4 May 1926	n/a
Poplar (DLR)	33C2	31 August 1987	Open	n/a

Station	Map ref	Opened	Closed (passengers)	Closed (freight)
Poplar Docks	33C2	1851	n/a	1981
Portland Road	*see Great Portland Street; renamed 1917*			
Post Office	*see St Paul's; renamed 1 February 1937*			
Preston Road (first)	17B1	21 May 1908	3 January 1932	n/a
Preston Road (second)	17B1	3 January 1932	Open	n/a
Preston Road Halt for Uxendon & Kenton	*see Preston Road Halt; renamed date unknown*			
Price's Siding	17G3	unknown	n/a	unknown
Primrose Hill	19F1	5 May 1855	28 September 1992	n/a
	Note: Station closed 1 January 1917 to 10 July 1922			
Prince Regent	34C5	28 March 1994	Open	n/a
Princess Royal Distribution Centre	17F2	1996	n/a	Open
Pudding Mill Lane	21F2	15 January 1996	Open	n/a
Putney Bridge	30D1	1 March 1880	Open	n/a
Putney Bridge & Fulham	*see Putney Bridge; renamed Putney Bridge & Hurlingham 1 September 1902*			
Putney Bridge & Hurlingham	*see Putney Bridge; renamed 1932*			
Quaker Oats (Southall)	27D5	unknown	n/a	unknown
Queens Park	18G3	2 June 1879	Open	6 July 1964
Queens Park (West Kilburn)	*see Queens Park; renamed December 1954*			
Queens Road	20D3	Never	n/a	n/a
Queen's Road	*see Queensway; renamed 1 September 1946*			
Queensbury	6F2	16 December 1934	Open	n/a
Queensway	30C2	30 July 1900	Open	n/a
Rainham	35A3	13 April 1854	Open	4 October 1965
Ravenscourt Park	29E5	1 April 1873	Open	n/a
Rayners Lane	15B5	26 May 1906	Open	10 August 1964
Rectory Road	20D3	27 May 1872	Open	n/a
Redbridge	22A5	14 December 1947	Open	
Refuse Transfer Station (Brentford)	28F2	1977	n/a	Open
Regent's Park	31A2	10 March 1906	Open	n/a
Ripple Lane Freightliner Terminal	23G2	1972	n/a	Open
Ripple Lane Yard	23G2	1937	n/a	Open
Roding Valley	11C4	3 February 1936	Open	n/a
Romford (GE)	24A5	18 June 1839	Open	unknown
	Note: Romford ex-GER and ex-MR stations amalgamated 2 April 1934			
Romford (Midland)	24A5	7 June 1893	Open	unknown
	Note: Romford ex-GER and ex-MR stations amalgamated 2 April 1934			
Romford, Victoria Road	24A4	1896	n/a	4 May 1970 *
Romford Brewery	24A5	unknown	n/a	unknown
Romford Gasworks	24B5	unknown	n/a	unknown
Rotherhithe	32D2	7 December 1869	Open	n/a
Royal Albert	34C5	28 March 1994	Open	n/a
Royal Mint Street (goods)	32C3	1853	n/a	1951
Royal Oak	30B1	30 October 1871	Open	n/a
Royal Small Arms Factory	3E4	unknown	n/a	unknown
Royal Victoria	33C4	28 March 1994	Open	n/a
Rugby Road Halt	29D4	8 April 1909	1 January 1917	n/a
Ruislip (LUL)	15C1	4 July 1904	Open	10 August 1964
Ruislip & Ickenham	*see West Ruislip; renamed 30 June 1947*			
Ruislip Depot (No 4MU)	14C1	1918	n/a	25 September 1969
Ruislip Gardens (GW/GC)	15D2	9 July 1934	21 July 1958	n/a
Ruislip Gardens (LUL)	15D2	21 November 1948	Open	n/a
Ruislip Manor	15D2	5 August 1912	Open	n/a
	Note: Station closed 12 February 1917 to 1 April 1919			
Ruislip Manor Halt	*see Ruislip Manor; renamed date unknown*			
Russell Square	31A4 / 38C3	15 December 1906	Open	n/a
St Ann's Road	20A4	2 October 1882	9 August 1942	n/a
St James Street, Walthamstow	20A1	26 April 1870	Open	n/a
St James's Park	31D3	24 December 1868	Open	n/a
St John's Wood Road	*see Lords; renamed St John's Wood 1 April 1925*			
St John's Wood	18G1	20 November 1939	Open	n/a
St John's Wood	*see Lords; renamed 11 June 1939*			
St Margaret's (LSWR)	37C4	2 October 1876	Open	n/a
St Mary's	*see St Mary's, Whitechapel Road; renamed 26 January 1923*			
St Mary's, Whitechapel Road	32B3	3 March 1884	1 May 1938	n/a
St Pancras	*see St Pancras International; renamed 6 November 2007*			
St Pancras (goods)	19F3	1867	n/a	2 June 1975
St Pancras International	19G3 / 38A3	1 October 1868	Open	n/a
St Paul's Thameslink	*see City Thameslink; renamed 30 September 1991*			
St Paul's (BR)	*see Blackfriars (BR); renamed 1 February 1937*			
St Paul's (LUL)	32B5 / 39D4	30 July 1900	Open	n/a
St Quintin Park & Wormwood Scrubs (first)	30B5	1 August 1871	1 November 1893	n/a
St Quintin Park & Wormwood Scrubs (second)	30B5	1 November 1893	3 October 1940	n/a
Sanderson & Son's Siding	16G2	unknown	n/a	unknown
Sandy Lodge	*see Moor Park; renamed Moor Park & Sandy Lodge 18 October 1923*			
Seven Kings	22C1	1 March 1899	Open	n/a
Seven Sisters (GE)	20A4	22 July 1872	Open	n/a
Seven Sisters (LUL)	20A4	1 September 1968	Open	n/a
Seven Sisters Road	*see Finsbury Park; renamed 15 November 1869*			
Shadwell (BR)	32C2	1 October 1840	7 July 1941	n/a
	Note: Station closed 22 May 1916 to 5 May 1919			
Shadwell (DLR)	31C2	31 August 1987	Open	n/a
Shadwell (EL)	32C2	10 April 1876	Open	n/a
Shadwell & St George's-in-the-East (EL)	*see Shadwell; '& St George's-in-the-East' carried 1 July 1900 to 1918*			
Shaftesbury Road	*see Ravenscourt Park; renamed 1 March 1888*			
Shepherds Bush (BR)	30D4	1 November 1869	21 October 1940	n/a
	Note: Station closed 21 October 1940 to 28 September 2008			
Shepherd's Bush (first)	30D4	27 May 1844	1 December 1844	n/a

Station	Map ref	Opened	Closed (passengers)	Closed (freight)
Shepherd's Bush (LUL — Central)	30D4	30 July 1900	Open	n/a
Shepherd's Bush (LUL — H&C) (first)	30D5	13 June 1864	1 April 1914	n/a
Shepherd's Bush (LUL — H&C) (second)	*see Shepherd's Bush Market; renamed 12 October 2008*			
Shepherd's Bush (second)	30D5	1 May 1874	5 June 1916	n/a
Shepherd's Bush Market	30D5	1 April 1914	Open	n/a
Shern Hall Street, Walthamstow	10G1	26 April 1870	17 November 1873	n/a
Shoreditch	*see Bishopsgate; renamed 27 July 1846*			
Shoreditch (EL)	32A3 / 39A2	10 April 1876	9 June 2006	n/a
Shoreditch High Street	32A3 / 39A2	2010	Open	n/a
Silver Street	10D5	22 July 1872	n/a	n/a
Silvertown	*see Silvertown & London City Airport; renamed 4 October 1987*			
Silvertown & London City Airport	34D4	19 June 1863	9 December 2006	5 May 1967 *
Sloane Square	31E1	24 December 1868	Open	n/a
Smallberry Green	28G3	22 August 1848	1 February 1850	n/a
Smithfield (G)	31B5 / 39A2	3 May 1869	n/a	30 July 1962
Smiths Siding	36E3	unknown	n/a	unknown
Snaresbrook	21A4	22 August 1856	Open	1 August 1949
Snaresbrook & Wanstead	*see Snaresbrook; '& Wanstead' carried November 1898 to 14 December 1947*			
Snow Hill	*see Holborn Viaduct Low Level; renamed 1 May 1912*			
Somers Town (goods)	19G3 / 38A2	1887	n/a	5 June 1967
South Acton (BR)	29D3	1 January 1880	Open	n/a
South Acton (LUL)	29D3	13 June 1905	2 March 1959	n/a
South Bromley	33B2	1 September 1884	23 April 1945	n/a
South Dock	33D2	18 December 1871	4 May 1926	n/a
South Ealing	28D1	1 May 1883	Open	n/a
South Greenford Halt	*see South Greenford; suffix dropped 5 May 1969*			
South Greenford	16G3	20 September 1926	Open	n/a
South Hampstead	18F1	2 June 1879	Open	n/a
	Note: Station closed 1 January 1917 to 10 July 1922; renamed South Hampstead on reopening			
South Harefield Halt	14B3	24 September 1928	1 October 1931	n/a
South Harrow & Roxeth	*see Northolt Park; renamed 13 May 1929*			
South Harrow (first)	*see Sudbury Hill, Harrow; renamed 19 July 1926*			
South Harrow (second)	16D4	5 July 1935	Open	n/a
South Harrow Gas Works	16C4	1910	n/a	1954
South Kensington (Dis)	30E1	10 July 1871	Open	n/a
South Kensington (Dis; ex-Met)	30E1	24 December 1868	Open	n/a
South Kentish Town	19E2	22 June 1907	5 June 1924	n/a
South Kenton	26C1	3 July 1933	Open	n/a
South Quay	33D2	31 August 1987	Open	n/a
South Ruislip & Northolt Junction	*see South Ruislip (GW/GC); renamed 30 June 1947*			
South Ruislip (GW/GC)	15D3	1 May 1908	Open	27 January 1964 *
South Ruislip (LUL)	15D3	21 November 1948	Open	n/a
South Tottenham & Stamford Hill	*see South Tottenham; renamed 1 July 1903*			
South Tottenham	20A3	1 May 1871	Open	4 July 1966
South Woodford (George Lane)	*see South Woodford; '(George Lane)' dropped 14 December 1947*			
South Woodford	11F3	22 August 1856	Open	1964
Southall	27D5	1 May 1839	Open	2 January 1967 *
Southall (Brentford) Gas Works	27D3	1868	n/a	1965
Southbury	3F1	21 November 1960	Open	n/a
Southgate (LUL)	9B1	13 March 1933	Open	n/a
Southgate & Colney Hatch	*see New Southgate; renamed New Southgate & Colney Hatch 1 October 1876*			
Spitalfields	32A3	Unknown	n/a	6 November 1967
Squirrels Heath & Guide Park	*see Gidea Park; renamed Gidea Park & Squirrels Heath 1 October 1913*			
Stamford Hill	20B4	22 July 1872	Open	n/a
Stamford Brook	29E5	1 February 1912	Open	n/a
Stanmore (LNW)	*see Stanmore Village; renamed 25 September 1950*			
Stanmore (LUL)	6C3	10 December 1932	Open	31 March 1936
Stanmore Village	6D4	18 December 1890	15 September 1952	6 July 1964
Star Lane	33A3	2010	Open	n/a
Stepney	*see Limehouse (second); renamed Stepney East 1 July 1923*			
Stepney East	*see Limehouse (second); renamed 11 May 1987*			
Stepney Green	32A1	23 June 1902	Open	n/a
Stoke Newington	20C4	27 May 1872	Open	7 December 1964
Stonebridge Park (first)	*see Harlesden (first); renamed 1 February 1901*			
Stonebridge Park (second)	17F2	15 June 1912	Open	June 1951
	Note: Station closed 9 January 1917 to 1 August 1917			
Stora Enso	23G2	unknown	n/a	Open
Strand (first)	*see Aldwych; renamed 9 May 1915*			
Strand (second)	*see Charing Cross (LUL — Northern); renamed 1 May 1979*			
Stratford (DLR)	21F3	To open 2010	Open	n/a
Stratford (HL)	21E1	20 June 1839	Open	n/a
Stratford (LL)	21F1	16 October 1854	Open	n/a
Stratford Bridge	*see Stratford Market (first); renamed 1 November 1880*			
Stratford International	21E2	13 December 2009	Open	n/a
Stratford Market (first)	21F3	14 June 1847	1992	n/a
Stratford Market (second)	21F3	1892	6 May 1957	n/a
Stratford Market (West Ham)	*see Stratford Market (second)/'(West Ham)' carried from 1898 to 1923*			
Stratford Market Goods	21F3	c1880	n/a	unknown
Strawberry Hill	37E3	1 December 1873	Open	n/a
Stroud Green	19B4	11 April 1881	5 July 1954	n/a
	Note: Station closed 29 October 1951 to 7 January 1952			
Sudbury (LNWR)	*see Wembley Central; renamed Sudbury & Wembley 1 May 1882*			
Sudbury & Harrow Road	16E2	1 March 1906	Open	3 May 1965
	Note: Station closed 22 September 1990 to 7 October 1990			
Sudbury Hill	16D3	28 June 1903	Open	n/a
Sudbury Hill, Harrow	16D3	1 March 1906	Open	3 May 1965
Sudbury & Wembley	*see Wembley Central; renamed Wembley for Sudbury 1 November 1910*			
Sudbury Town	16E2	28 June 1903	Open	n/a
Swiss Cottage (LUL - Met)	18E1	13 April 1868	18 August 1940	n/a
Swiss Cottage (LUL)	18E1	20 November 1939	Open	n/a
Syon Lane	28G2	5 July 1931	Open	n/a

Station	Map ref	Opened	Closed (passengers)	Closed (freight)
Tarmac (Hayes)	27D2	Unknown	n/a	Open
Taylor's Lane Power Station	17F4	1903	n/a	March 1972
Teddington	37G3	1 July 1863	Open	3 May 1965
Teddington (Bushey Park)	*see Teddington; renamed Teddington & Bushey Park July 1908*			
Teddington & Bushey Park	*see Teddington; renamed August 1911*			
Temple	31C4 / 38E4	30 May 1870	Open	n/a
Temple Mills Yard	21D2	1959	n/a	Open
Thames Wharf	33C4	1846	n/a	4 October 1965 *
The Hale	*see Mill Hill (The Hale); renamed 1 March 1928*			
The Hale Halt	*see Mill Hill (The Hale); renamed The Hale, May 1912*			
The Monument	*see Monument; renamed Monument by 1904*			
The Temple	*see Temple; renamed Temple date unknown*			
Theobalds Grove	3A3	1 October 1891	Open	1967
	Note: Station closed 1 October 1909 to 1 March 1915 and 1 July 1919 to 21 November 1960			
Tidal Basin	33C4	1858	15 August 1943	n/a
Torrington Park	*see Woodside Park; renamed Torrington Park, Woodside 1 May 1872*			
Torrington Park, Woodside	*see Woodside Park; renamed Woodside Park 1 May 1882*			
Tottenham	*see Tottenham Hale; known as Tottenham 15 September 1840 until June 1875 and from November 1938 until 1 December 1968*			
Tottenham Court Road (LUL — Central)	31B3 / 38D2	30 July 1900	Open	n/a
Tottenham Court Road (LUL — Northern) (first)		*see Goodge Street; renamed 9 March 1908*		
Tottenham Court Road (LUL — Northern) (second)	31B3 / 38D2	22 June 1907	Open	n/a
Tottenham Gasworks	10D4	unknown	n/a	unknown
Tottenham Hale (GE)	10G4	15 September 1840	Open	n/a
Tottenham Hale (LUL)	10G5	1 September 1968	Open	n/a
Totteridge & Whetstone	8B4	1 April 1872	Open	1 October 1962
Totteridge	*see Totteridge & Whetstone; renamed 1 April 1874*			
Tower Gateway	32C4 / 39E1	31 August 1987	Open	n/a
	Note: Station closed 30 June 2008 to 2 March 2009			
Tower Hill (first)	32C4 / 39E1	6 October 1884	5 February 1967	n/a
Tower Hill (second)	32C4 / 39E1	25 September 1882	Open	n/a
	Note: Station closed 13 October 1884 to 5 February 1967			
Tower of London	*see Tower Hill (second); renamed and reopened 5 February 1967*			
Trafalgar Square	*see Charing Cross (LUL — Northern); renamed 12 September 1976*			
Trumper's Crossing Halt	28D4	2 May 1904	1 February 1926	n/a
	Note: Station closed between 22 March 1915 and 12 April 1920			
Tufnell Park	19D2	22 June 1907	Open	n/a
Turkey Street	3C2	21 November 1960	Open	*see Forty Hill*
Turnham Green	29E4	1 January 1869	Open±	n/a
Turnpike Lane	20B5	19 September 1932	Open	n/a
Twickenham (first)	37D3	22 August 1848	28 March 1954	n/a
Twickenham (second)	37D3	28 March 1954	Open	2 January 1967
Twyford Abbey Ammunition Store	29A3	unknown	n/a	unknown
Twyford Abbey Halt	29A1	1 May 1904	1 May 1911	n/a
Upminster	25C2	1 May 1885	Open	7 December 1964
Upminster Bridge	24C1	17 December 1934	Open	n/a
Upney	22F1	12 September 1932	Open	n/a
Upper Holloway	19C3	21 July 1868	Open	7 May 1968
Upton Park (BR)	22F5	17 September 1877	15 June 1962	n/a
Upton Park (LUL)	22F5	12 September 1932	Open	n/a
Upton Park Goods	22F5	1895	n/a	1969
Uxbridge (MET) (first)	14F4	4 July 1904	4 December 1938	n/a
Uxbridge (MET) (second)	14F4	4 December 1938	1 May 1939	
Uxbridge Road	*see Shepherd's Bush (BR); station reopened and renamed 28 September 2008*			
Uxbridge Road Goods	30C4	1869	n/a	1967
Uxbridge High Street	14E4	1 May 1907	1 September 1939	24 February 1964
	Note: Station closed 1 January 1917 to 3 May 1920			
Uxbridge Vine Street	14F4	8 September 1856	10 September 1962	24 February 1964
Uxbridge	*see Uxbridge Vine Street; renamed 1 May 1907*			
Vauxhall (LUL)	31F4	23 July 1971	Open	n/a
Victoria (BR)	31E2	1 October 1860	Open	n/a
Victoria (LUL - Dis)	31D2	24 December 1968	Open	n/a
Victoria (LUL - Vic)	31D2	7 March 1969	Open	n/a
Victoria Docks	33C5	1855	n/a	c1967
Victoria Park & Bow	21G1	2 April 1849	6 January 1851	n/a
Walham Green	*see Fulham Broadway; renamed 1 March 1952*			
Waltham (first)	*see Waltham Cross (first); renamed 1 December 1882*			
Waltham Cross & Abbey	*see Waltham Cross (second); '& Abbey' carried 1 May 1894 to 20 February 1969*			
Waltham Cross (second)	3A3	1885	Open	n/a
Waltham Cross (first)	3A3	1842	1885	n/a
Waltham Cross Gas Works	3A3	unknown	n/a	unknown
Walthamstow Central (BR)	21A1	26 April 1870	Open	2 November 1964 *
Walthamstow Central (LUL)	21A1	1 September 1968	n/a	
Walthamstow Queen's Road	21A1	9 July 1894	Open	6 May 1968
Walthamstow	*see Walthamstow Queen's Road; renamed 6 May 1968*			
Wanstead	21A5	14 December 1947	Open	n/a
Wanstead Park	21D5	9 July 1894	Open	n/a
Wapping	32C2	7 December 1869	Open	n/a
Wapping & Shadwell	*see Wapping; renamed 10 April 1876*			
Warren Street (LUL — Victoria)	31A3 / 38B1	7 March 1969	Open	n/a
Warren Street (LUL — Northern)	31A3 / 38B1	22 June 1907	Open	n/a
Warwick Avenue	30A2	31 January 1915	Open	n/a
Water Lane	*see Angel Road; renamed 1 January 1864*			
Waterloo (BR)	31D4 / 38G1	13 July 1848	Open	n/a
Waterloo International	38G5	14 November 1994	13 November 2007	n/a
	Note: Platform 20 being integrated within the domestic station			
Waterloo (LUL – Bakerloo)	31D4 / 38G5	10 March 1906	Open	n/a
Waterloo (LUL – Northern)	31D4 / 38G5	13 September 1926	Open	n/a

London North

Station	Map ref	Opened	Closed (passengers)	Closed (freight)
Waterloo (LUL – Jubilee)	31D4 / 38G5	24 September 1999	Open	n/a
Waterloo (LUL – W&C)	31D4 / 38G5	8 August 1898	Open	n/a
	Note: Waterloo & City line closed for refurbishment and other reasons on a number of occasions including 14 December 1940-3 March 1941;			
	11 May 1941-26 May 1941; 8 August 1992-6 September 1992; 29 May 1993-19 July 1993; 31 March 1994-5 April 1994; and,			
	1 April 2006-11 September 2006. Line transferred to LUL 1 April 1994.			
Welsh Harp	17B5	2 May 1870	1 July 1903	n/a
Wembley Central	17E1	1842	Open	4 January 1965
Wembley Complex	see Wembley Stadium (second); renamed Wembley Stadium 11 May 1987			
Wembley Exhibition	see Wembley Stadium (first); renamed by February 1928			
Wembley Exhibition (Goods)	17D2	unknown	n/a	3 December 1962
Wembley Hill	see Wembley Stadium (second); renamed Wembley Complex 8 May 1978			
Wembley Park	17C2	12 May 1894	5 July 1965	
Wembley Stadium (second)	17E2	1 March 1906	Open	n/a
Wembley Stadium (first)	17D2	28 April 1923	1 September 1969	n/a
Wembley for Sudbury	see Wembley Central; renamed 5 July 1948			
West Acton	29B2	5 November 1923	Open	n/a
West Brompton (LUL)	30F3	12 April 1869	Open	n/a
West Brompton (BR)	30F3	1 September 1866	Open	n/a
	Note: Station closed 21 October 1940 to 1 June 1999			
West Drayton (first)	26C6	4 June 1838	9 August 1884	n/a
West Drayton (second)	26C3	9 August 1884	Open	Open
West Drayton & Yiewsley	see West Drayton (second): '& Yiewsley' carried 1895 to 6 May 1974			
West Drayton (Air Ministry) Depot	26D3	c1918	n/a	unknown
West Drayton Coal (Celtic Energy)	26C4	1963	n/a	1999
West Ealing	28C2	1 March 1871	Open	1978
West Ealing New Goods	28C2	3 February 1908	n/a	23 May 1980
West End Lane	see West Hampstead (second); renamed 5 May 1975			
West End	see West Hampstead Thameslink; renamed West End & Brondesbury 1 April 1904			
West End & Brondesbury	see West Hampstead Thameslink; renamed West Hampstead (first) 1 September 1905			
West End Sidings	18E3	1868	n/a	1968
West Ferry	33C1	31 August 1987	Open	n/a
West Finchley	8D5	1 March 1933	Open	n/a
West Green	9G4	1 January 1878	7 January 1963	5 October 1964
West Ham (first)	21G3	1 February 1901	Open	n/a
West Ham (second)	33A3	14 May 1979	9 December 2006	n/a
	Note: Station closed 29 May 1994 to 29 October 1995; being rebuilt as part of DLR extension			
West Ham Manor Road	see West Ham (first); 'Manor Road' carried 11 February 1924 to 1 January 1969			
West Hampstead (first)	see West Hampstead Thameslink; renamed West Hampstead Midland 25 September 1950			
West Hampstead (second)	18E3	1 March 1888	Open	2 January 1967
West Hampstead Midland	see West Hampstead Thameslink; renamed 1988			
West Hampstead Thameslink	18E2	1 March 1871	Open	unknown
West Harrow	16B5	17 November 1913	Open	n/a
West India Dock, Southside	33D2	unknown	unknown	unknown
West India Docks	33C	16 July 1840	4 May 1926	n/a
West India Quay	33C1	31 August 1987	Open	n/a
	Note: Station closed 14 October 1991 to 28 June 1993			
West Kensington	30E3	9 September 1874	Open	n/a
West Kensington (goods)	30F3	1878	n/a	14 July 1965
West London Waste	15E4	Unknown	n/a	Open
West Ruislip	14C1	2 April 1906	Open	6 October 1975
West Silverton (DLR)	33C5	2 December 2005	Open	n/a
Westbourne Park (BR)	30B3	30 October 1871	13 March 1992	n/a
Westbourne Park (LUL)	30B3	1 February 1866	Open	n/a
Westminster (LUL — District)	31D4	24 December 1868	Open	n/a
Westminster (LUL — Jubilee)	31D4	22 November 1999	Open	n/a
Westminster Bridge	see Westminster (LUL — District); renamed 1907			
White City (LUL — Central)	30C5	23 November 1947	Open	n/a
White City (LUL — H&C)	30C5	1 May 1908	25 October 1959	n/a
	Note: Station closed 1 November 1914 to 23 November 1947			
White Hart Lane	9E5	22 July 1872	Open	2 July 1977
Whitechapel (EL)	32B2	10 April 1876	Open n/a	
Whitechapel (LUL)	32B2	6 October 1884	Open	n/a
Whitechapel (Mile End)	see Whitechapel (LUL); renamed 13 November 1901			
Whitecross Street (goods)	32B5	Unknown	n/a	1 March 1936
Whitton	37D1	6 July 1930	Open	n/a
Willesden	17G4	1842	1 September 1866	n/a
Willesden (HL)	17G4	1866	1885	n/a
Willesden & Dudden Hill	see Dudding Hill; renamed 1875			
Willesden Green	18E4	24 November 1879	Open 3 January 1966	
Willesden Green & Cricklewood	see Willesden Green; '& Cricklewood' carried 1 June 1894 to 1938			
Willesden Junction (High Level)	17G5	1 September 1866	Open	n/a
Willesden Junction (Main Line)	17G5	1 September 1866	3 December 1962	n/a
Willesden Junction (New)	17G5	15 June 1912	Open	n/a
Willesden Power Station	17G3	unknown	n/a	unknown
Winchmore Hill	9A3	1 April 1871	Open	1 October 1962
Wood Green (GNR)	see Alexandra Palace; renamed 17 May 1982			
Wood Green (Alexandra Palace)	see Alexandra Palace; suffix carried 1 June 1864 to 18 March 1971			
Wood Green (LUL)	9F2	19 September 1932	Open	n/a
Wood Lane (LUL — Central)	30C4	14 May 1908	23 November 1947	n/a
Wood Lane (LUL — H&C) (first)	see White City (LUL — H&C); renamed and reopened 23 November 1947			
Wood Lane (LUL — H&C) (second)	30C5	12 October 2008	Open	n/a
Wood Street	10G1	17 November 1873	Open	6 May 1968
Wood Street, Walthamstow	see Wood Street; renamed 18 March 1971			
Woodford	11D3	22 August 1856	Open	18 April 1966
Woodgrange Park	22E5	9 July 1894	Open	7 December 1964
Woodside Park	8C4	1 April 1872	Open	1 October 1962
Woodstock Road Halt	29D4	8 April 1909	1 January 1917	n/a
Woolwich Arsenal (DLR)	34D2	10 January 2009	Open	n/a
Wormwood Scrubs	see St Quintin Park & Wormwood Scrubs (first); renamed 1 August 1892			
York Road	19F4	15 December 1906	19 September 1932	n/a

* Closed for all goods traffic except private sidings; these closed later.